I CAN'T

Strategies To Overcoming Your Limiting Beliefs

By

Anthony Brown

ISBN: 979-8-9949097-0-6

Second Edition

Published by
Eleven Legacy Press

For permissions or inquiries, contact:
INSERT SOMETHING HERE OR DELETE THIS SECTION.

Redefining Success. Realigning Purpose. Releasing Potential.

TABLE OF CONTENTS

INTRODUCTION 6

CHAPTER ONE...8

    UNDERSTANDING LIMITING BELIEFS 8

    The Nature of Limiting Beliefs 10

    Origin of Limiting Beliefs..11

    The Impact of Limiting Beliefs 13

Limiting Beliefs: The Invisible Chains 15

The Power of Limiting Beliefs in Shaping Reality 16

Why Awareness Is the Key to Breaking Free 19

CHAPTER TWO 23

THE NEUROSCIENCE OF BELIEF 23

The Influence of Past Experiences, Emotions, and Environmental Factors 23

Belief Formation 26

How Beliefs Are Formed and Reinforced 28

The Role of Emotions in Belief Formation and the Prefrontal Cortex......................30

Environmental Factors and the Role of the Prefrontal Cortex in Belief Formation 30

Changing Beliefs Through Brain Rewiring 34

Practical Strategies for Harnessing the Neuroscience of Belief 39

CHAPTER THREE 42

IDENTIFYING LIMITING BELIEFS 42

The Origins of Limiting Beliefs 44

The Process of Identifying Limiting Beliefs 47

The Impact of Limiting Beliefs 48

Identifying Your Own Limiting Beliefs 50

CHAPTER FOUR 53

CHALLENGING AND REFRAMING BELIEFS 53

Challenging Limiting Beliefs 53

Challenging Negative Self-Talk 57

Challenging the Validity of Beliefs 59

Reframing Limiting Beliefs 61

Technique To Reframe Limiting Beliefs 64

CHAPTER FIVE 68

THE POWER OF MINDSET SHIFTS 68

How Mindset Influences Behavior 71

Adopting a Growth Mindset 73

Challenge Strong Beliefs 74

CHAPTER SIX 78

ACTIONABLE STRATEGIES FOR CHANGE 78

The Nature of Change..78

Assessing the Need for Change 80

How Beliefs and Mindsets Affect Change 82

The Role of Mindset in Embracing Change 85

Actionable Strategies for Change 86

Time Management and Productivity Strategies 88

CHAPTER SEVEN 94

BUILDING RESILIENCE AND OVERCOMING SETBACKS 94

Importance of Resilience in Daily Life 95

Characteristics of Resilient Individuals 96

Building Resilience 99

Harnessing the Power of Resilience 100

CHAPTER EIGHT 104

EMBRACING EMPOWERING BELIEFS 104

Understanding Empowering Beliefs 104

Characteristics of Empowering Beliefs 106

The Influence of Beliefs and Mindset on Empowerment 107

Embracing Empowering Beliefs 109

The Path Forward: Empowering Beliefs in Action..111

The Impact of Self-Confidence Beliefs on Personal Growth 112

CHAPTER NINE 115

CREATING A SUPPORTIVE ENVIRONMENT 115

Understanding the Importance of a Supportive Environment 115

The Influence of Beliefs and Mindsets on a Supportive Environment..................117

Building a Supportive Environment 119

The Power of Beliefs and Mindsets 120

How a Supportive Environment Impacts Personal Growth 122

CHAPTER TEN 126

THE JOURNEY OF CONTINUOUS GROWTH 126

Understanding Continuous Growth 127

How Beliefs and Mindsets Influence Continuous Growth 128

The Continuous Growth Journey 129

The Impact of Continuous Growth on Personal Empowerment 131

CONCLUSION 134

EMBRACING YOUR LIMITLESS POTENTIAL 134

Understanding Infinite Potential 134

How Beliefs and Mindsets Influence Our Infinite Potential 136

Embrace Your Infinite Potential 137

How Infinite Potential Impacts Personal Growth 139

INTRODUCTION

The Power of Belief

Belief is a remarkable force. It drives human potential, influencing how we perceive ourselves and navigate the world. It shapes our thoughts, guides our actions, and defines the limits of what we think is possible. At its core, belief is deeply personal, capable of propelling us toward greatness or confining us within doubt and fear. Belief shapes our reality. It's the lens through which we interpret experiences and the compass directing our choices. Our beliefs can empower us to chase dreams with courage and determination, or they can trap us in cycles of self-doubt. Understanding belief's power is essential for unlocking personal growth.

Belief is the invisible engine that drives our actions, decisions, and ultimately, our lives. It's the force that quietly determines whether we aim high or settle for less, whether we push through challenges or give up when things get tough. Whether you realize it or not, your beliefs about yourself and your world shape every aspect of your experience. They define what you think is possible and, more importantly, what you think is impossible. Think of belief as the lens through which you see the world. For some, it's a lens of opportunity—one that shows them possibilities and fuels their ambitions. For others, it's a filter of limitation, casting shadows of doubt and fear on even the brightest dreams. But here's the truth: that lens can be changed. And when it does, the entire landscape of your life changes with it. Beliefs can either be a cage that keeps you stuck or a key that unlocks your potential. When you believe in your abilities, you're more likely to take risks, persevere through challenges, and see opportunities where others see obstacles.

We've all heard stories of people who defied the odds—who rose from seemingly impossible circumstances to accomplish things no one thought they could. What made the difference? It wasn't luck or random chance. It was belief. A belief in their potential, their abilities, and their worth. That belief fueled their perseverance, helped them see opportunities instead of obstacles, and pushed them to keep going even when everything seemed stacked against them.

Why Beliefs Matter More Than We Realize

Beliefs are the invisible scripts running in the background of your mind, subtly influencing how you see the world and your place in it. They guide how you interpret experiences and often determine how far you'll allow yourself to go. Consider this: two people can face the exact same challenge, yet one will rise to the occasion, while the other will shrink back in fear. What's the difference? It's not intelligence or talent. It's belief—what they believe about themselves, their capabilities, and the situation at hand.

Positive beliefs can be empowering, but negative or limiting beliefs are like chains that hold you back. Think about the phrases that might echo in your mind:

- ❖ "I'm not smart enough to do that."

- ❖ "I could never be successful."

- ❖ "I'm just not the type of person who takes risks."

Each of these thoughts is a belief. And as long as you continue to believe them, they'll become self-fulfilling prophecies. That's why, to truly unlock your potential, it's essential to break through those limiting beliefs and replace them with empowering ones. Imagine if you could change the way you think about yourself and what you're capable of. What if the goals that once felt out of reach suddenly seemed achievable? The truth is, the power to transform your life is already inside of you—embedded in your beliefs. And the most amazing part is that beliefs aren't fixed; they can be changed, reshaped, and reprogrammed.

As you begin this journey, remember that the power of belief is already inside you. It's there, ready to be used to create the life you've always dreamed of. Embrace the path, trust in the power of your beliefs, and unlock the endless possibilities that await you. In the upcoming chapters, we'll dive into the connection between belief, resilience, and personal growth. Through real-life stories, science, and practical strategies, we'll discover how to challenge limiting beliefs and strengthen your resilience, giving you the tools to thrive no matter what life throws your way.

CHAPTER ONE

UNDERSTANDING LIMITING BELIEFS

Limiting beliefs are like invisible chains that hold us back, invisible barriers that prevent us from reaching our full potential. These beliefs manifest as whispers of doubt that tell us we are not good enough or capable of succeeding. To free ourselves from their control and begin on the path of personal growth and self-determination, we must first understand their nature, origin, and impact on our lives.

Limiting beliefs are the negative thoughts, assumptions, or attitudes we hold about ourselves and the world that place boundaries on our potential. They are the mental barriers that prevent us from taking action, achieving goals, or pursuing our true passions. These beliefs are often deeply ingrained and operate beneath our conscious awareness, shaping our behavior and influencing our decisions in powerful ways.

Limiting beliefs can manifest in statements like:

- ❖ "I'm not smart enough to succeed."

- ❖ "I don't deserve happiness."

- ❖ "I'm too old to start something new."

- ❖ "This is just the way things are."

At their core, limiting beliefs create an internal narrative that restricts personal growth, convincing us that we are incapable of more. They build invisible walls around our possibilities, keeping us in a comfort zone that feels safe but also keeps us from experiencing the fullness of life. Over time, these beliefs lead to self-doubt, fear, and hesitation, preventing us from stepping into opportunities and reaching our full potential.

Limiting beliefs are the self-imposed mental boundaries we create, shaping our perceptions, actions, and potential. These beliefs stem from experiences, societal influences, and personal narratives, and they serve as roadblocks, limiting our ability to achieve our goals and reach our true potential. Limiting beliefs can exist in many forms, from small doubts that quietly erode confidence to deeply ingrained attitudes that shape every aspect of our lives. At their essence, limiting beliefs are assumptions about our capabilities, worth, or the world around us that keep us stuck in a cycle of underachievement, hesitation, and fear. They are the internal dialogue that holds us back from growth. Imagine wanting to pursue a promotion at work but hearing a voice in your head say, "I'm not good enough," or having dreams of starting a business but constantly thinking, "I'm not capable of being successful." These thoughts become barriers to taking action, causing us to feel stuck, limited, or unworthy of our desires.

The Nature of Limiting Beliefs

Limiting beliefs are deeply ingrained perceptions that shape our reality by restricting what we think we can achieve. These beliefs are often so embedded in our subconscious that we fail to recognize them, yet they dictate much of our behavior. They act as invisible barriers, holding us back from taking risks, pursuing opportunities, and realizing our full potential. Operating in the background, limiting beliefs manifest through fear, doubt, and negative self-talk; subtly influencing how we view ourselves and the world around us. Whether we're aware of them or not, these beliefs keep us in a mental prison, restricting our ability to explore new possibilities or step outside our comfort zone.

A significant aspect of limiting beliefs is their unconscious nature. Because they often develop early in life—through past experiences, failures, or the influence of authority figures—limiting beliefs become part of the mental framework we use to interpret the world. For example, if you were told as a child that you weren't good at math, you might carry this belief into adulthood, automatically assuming you're incapable of handling anything related to numbers. This belief may prevent you from pursuing a career that involves quantitative skills or even handling personal finances with confidence. The danger is that we accept these beliefs as fact, without ever questioning their validity, thereby limiting our potential for growth.

Fear plays a central role in the formation of limiting beliefs, particularly the fear of failure. The fear of making mistakes or encountering setbacks creates a mindset where we avoid anything that challenges our abilities. Instead of seeing failure as an opportunity for learning, we equate it with personal inadequacy. This belief keeps us stuck in our comfort zones, unwilling to try new things or push ourselves. For instance, someone who fears failure might avoid starting a new business or learning a new skill because they're afraid of not succeeding. Ironically, by avoiding these risks, they also miss out on opportunities for growth and progress.

Another prevalent form of limiting belief stems from the fear of judgment or evaluation by others. Many people prioritize the opinions of others over their own goals and aspirations, conforming to societal expectations rather than pursuing what truly fulfills them. For example, someone who has a passion for the arts may be discouraged by societal pressures that favor more traditional career paths, such as medicine or law. Out of fear of criticism or disapproval, they may suppress their creative talents, believing that pursuing their true passion is unrealistic or not valuable. This fear of judgment forces individuals to live in authentically, further reinforcing limiting beliefs.

Ultimately, limiting beliefs shape our mindset in ways that often go unnoticed, but they have a profound impact on our decisions and life paths. By internalizing these beliefs, we unknowingly set boundaries on what we think we can achieve. The key to overcoming limiting beliefs is recognizing them, challenging their origins, and actively working to replace them with empowering beliefs that open up new possibilities. Breaking free from limiting beliefs allows us to step into our true potential, take risks with confidence, and embrace personal growth.

Origin of Limiting Beliefs

Limiting beliefs often originate from a complex interplay of personal experiences, social influences, and environmental factors that shape our worldview from a young age. These beliefs are not innate; rather, they develop over time as we navigate our interactions with family, peers, educators, and society. Understanding the origins of limiting beliefs is crucial for unraveling their grip on our lives and paving the way for personal growth and transformation.

One significant source of limiting beliefs is our early childhood experiences. The messages we receive from parents and caregivers can profoundly influence how we perceive ourselves and our capabilities. For instance, a child who is frequently criticized or belittled may internalize the belief that they are not good enough or that they will never succeed. Conversely, a child who is overprotected and shielded from challenges may develop the belief that they are incapable of handling adversity. These formative years are critical; they set the groundwork for how we view our abilities and self-worth, often leading to self-limiting narratives that persist into adulthood.

Peer influence also plays a pivotal role in shaping limiting beliefs. During adolescence, individuals become increasingly aware of their social environment and the opinions of their peers. If a child is teased or ostracized for pursuing their interests or talents, they may develop a belief that it's safer to conform to group expectations rather than risk ridicule. This fear of social rejection can lead to a reluctance to explore one's passions or talents, reinforcing the notion that certain pursuits are off-limits. The desire to fit in can be a powerful motivator, leading individuals to abandon their dreams and settle for less than they are capable of achieving.

Societal norms and cultural expectations contribute significantly to the formation of limiting beliefs. Many cultures impose specific ideals regarding success, appearance, behavior, and gender roles. For instance, the belief that success is defined by wealth or social status can create pressure to conform to these standards, leading individuals to dismiss their unique strengths and talents. Similarly, cultural narratives around failure and success can instill fear, causing individuals to shy away from risks that could potentially lead to personal growth. When societal beliefs become internalized, they can severely restrict individual potential and hinder the pursuit of meaningful goals.

Negative life experiences, such as trauma or failure, can also give rise to limiting beliefs. When faced with setbacks, individuals may generalize these experiences, leading them to believe that they are incapable or unworthy of success in other areas of their lives. For example, someone who has experienced a significant professional setback may conclude that they are not cut out for leadership roles, even if they possess the skills and experience necessary to succeed. This kind of cognitive distortion can create a cycle of self-doubt and avoidance, further entrenching limiting beliefs.

Recognizing the origins of limiting beliefs is the first step toward dismantling them. By reflecting on past experiences and identifying how they have shaped our beliefs, we can begin to challenge these narratives. Understanding that limiting beliefs are learned rather than inherent empowers us to question their validity and replace them with more positive, constructive beliefs. This process of unlearning and reframing is essential for breaking free from the chains of self-imposed limitations and unlocking our true potential.

The Impact of Limiting Beliefs

Limiting beliefs have far-reaching effects on our lives. They shape our identity, affect our self-esteem, impact our relationships, and hinder our professional growth. Self-esteem and self-worth: Negative self-talk can erode confidence and lead to a feeling of inadequacy. People who believe they don't deserve happiness may engage in self-sabotaging behaviors and avoid fulfilling experiences. Understanding these impacts is crucial for recognizing how deeply embedded beliefs can dictate our behaviors and choices, ultimately keeping us from realizing our full potential.

1. **Self-Esteem and Self-Worth**

   At the core of many limiting beliefs lies a diminished sense of self-esteem and self-worth. Negative self-talk—those persistent whispers of inadequacy—can erode our confidence over time. Individuals who believe they are unworthy of happiness or success often find themselves engaging in self-sabotaging behaviors that reinforce these beliefs. For example, someone might procrastinate on important projects because they believe they are not capable of success, leading to missed opportunities and further reinforcing feelings of inadequacy. This cycle of negative self-perception can prevent individuals from pursuing fulfilling experiences, leaving them feeling stuck and unfulfilled. When we internalize beliefs that we are not enough, we effectively lock ourselves into a narrow view of our abilities and worth, diminishing our overall quality of life.

2. **Relationships and Social Interactions**

Limiting beliefs also significantly impact our relationships and social interactions. Beliefs about our worthiness can lead to feelings of unworthiness in the eyes of others, causing individuals to distance themselves emotionally. For example, someone who fears rejection may avoid vulnerability and intimacy, believing that they are undeserving of love or that they will inevitably be let down. This fear often results in shallow relationships and a lack of meaningful connections, fostering isolation and loneliness. Furthermore, when we project limiting beliefs onto our relationships, we can unintentionally push away those who genuinely care about us, creating a self-fulfilling prophecy that reinforces our beliefs about isolation and inadequacy. The result is a cycle of emotional distance that prevents us from forming deep, fulfilling bonds with others.

3. Career and Success

In the professional realm, limiting beliefs can be equally detrimental. Many individuals grapple with fear of failure and imposter syndrome, believing that they are not as competent or qualified as their peers. This perception often leads to avoidance of challenges and reluctance to seize new opportunities, stunting career growth and limiting success. For example, an employee who believes they are not suited for leadership roles may decline opportunities for advancement, ultimately hindering their professional development. This avoidance behavior not only restricts their career trajectory but also perpetuates the belief that they are incapable of achieving more. As a result, individuals may find themselves trapped in unfulfilling roles, feeling frustrated and unfulfilled while failing to recognize their potential for growth and advancement.

4. Emotional and Mental Well-Being

The impact of limiting beliefs extends beyond self-esteem, relationships, and career; they can also take a toll on our emotional and mental well-being. Constantly grappling with negative beliefs can lead to heightened anxiety, depression, and feelings of hopelessness. When individuals believe they cannot change their circumstances, they may become resigned to their situations, fostering a sense of helplessness. This emotional burden can drain energy and enthusiasm for life, making it difficult to engage in activities that once brought joy and fulfillment. By perpetuating a negative self-image, limiting beliefs can trap individuals in a cycle of despair, diminishing their overall well-being and quality of life.

Limiting Beliefs: The Invisible Chains

Limiting beliefs are like invisible chains that silently restrict us from realizing our true potential. Their power lies in their subtlety—they don't announce themselves boldly or loudly, but instead quietly infiltrate our minds, gradually shaping our thoughts, decisions, and behaviors. These beliefs create mental patterns that keep us locked in a state of inertia, making it difficult for us to move forward or break free from self-imposed limitations. The most dangerous aspect of limiting beliefs is that they often form early in life, during our most impressionable years. Whether it's through a negative experience, societal expectations, or comments from authority figures like parents, teachers, or peers, these beliefs begin to take root. For instance, a child who is told repeatedly that they aren't good at math might internalize this as a truth, which later morphs into the belief, "I'm not intelligent," or "I can't succeed in anything technical." This early programming becomes a lens through which future experiences are interpreted, reinforcing a pattern of self-doubt and avoidance.

What makes limiting beliefs so difficult to overcome is that they often seem rational or even protective. For example, someone who believes "I'm not good enough" may avoid taking risks in life, believing they are protecting themselves from failure or disappointment. This belief feels safe because it keeps them within their comfort zone, but it also traps them in mediocrity. Similarly, someone who thinks "I don't deserve love" might subconsciously sabotage relationships or avoid intimacy altogether, convincing themselves they're avoiding inevitable rejection, when in reality, they're limiting their capacity for deep connections.

Another reason limiting beliefs are so insidious is that they operate automatically. Over time, these beliefs become so deeply ingrained in our psyche that we stop questioning them. They feel like unchangeable facts rather than just perspectives that can be challenged. This leads to habitual behavior patterns, where we avoid opportunities for growth because of the fear, insecurity, or doubt that these beliefs have planted in our minds. They act as mental chains that bind us to past failures, negative experiences, or false narratives about who we are and what we can achieve.

Limiting beliefs often disguise themselves as protective mechanisms. For instance, if you've experienced rejection or failure in the past, a limiting belief might tell you, "Don't try again, you'll only fail." This belief creates a sense of comfort and safety, as it seems to prevent future pain. But in reality, it holds you back from the very opportunities that could lead to personal growth, fulfillment, and success. What feels like protection is actually a prison. These invisible chains are particularly hard to break because they often go unnoticed. We've lived with them for so long that we no longer see them as beliefs but as facts. We may not even be aware that these mental barriers are shaping our actions—or in many cases, our inaction. As a result, we operate within a narrow scope of possibility, never venturing outside of what we believe is possible for us.

For example, someone might dream of starting their own business but hold the limiting belief, "I'm not capable of running a successful company." They might take small steps toward their goal, but at every major decision point, this belief whispers doubt into their mind. They might hesitate to take on bigger projects, avoid networking with potential investors, or shy away from marketing their business, all because they are held back by an invisible chain that tells them they're not capable. In this way, limiting beliefs create a self-fulfilling prophecy—by believing they cannot succeed, they fail to take the necessary actions that could lead to success.

The Power of Limiting Beliefs in Shaping Reality

Limiting beliefs have a profound impact on how we perceive and navigate the world around us. They function like mental filters, distorting reality and shaping our experiences in ways that often reinforce negativity and self-doubt. When we operate under limiting beliefs, it's as if we're wearing a set of glasses with dark lenses— everything we see is colored by these negative assumptions, influencing how we interpret our experiences, evaluate opportunities, and respond to setbacks. Limiting beliefs dictate how we perceive ourselves and the world. These beliefs generate internal narratives that tell us we aren't capable, aren't worthy, or aren't deserving of success and happiness. Over time, this mindset starts to shape our reality in ways that create self-fulfilling prophecies. If we consistently tell ourselves that we aren't good enough to achieve something, we may stop trying altogether, or we may approach opportunities with such hesitation and doubt that our efforts fall short. This confirms the very belief we started with, reinforcing the idea that success isn't for us.

Imagine, for a moment, looking at life through a lens that constantly whispers, "You can't," "You're not good enough," or "It's too late for you." These messages become the backdrop against which every decision is made, every interaction is handled, and every opportunity is evaluated. When limiting beliefs filter our perception, even the most promising opportunities can appear risky or unattainable. We might not even recognize potential chances for growth because our belief system has already dismissed them as impossible or not meant for us.

For example, someone who believes they're not smart enough to succeed in a challenging career may decline a job promotion or avoid pursuing a higher degree, fearing they will inevitably fail. Despite external evidence of their competence, the internal voice fueled by their limiting belief holds more sway. As a result, they miss out on life-changing opportunities, not because they aren't capable, but because they believe they aren't.

This distorted perception of reality also affects how we interpret setbacks. When things don't go as planned, individuals operating under limiting beliefs may see these failures as proof that they're inadequate. Instead of viewing challenges as opportunities to learn and grow, they reinforce the idea that failure is confirmation of their shortcomings. They tell themselves, "See, I knew I wasn't good enough" or "This always happens to me," which further entrenches the limiting belief. In contrast, individuals who don't operate under the weight of limiting beliefs may interpret setbacks differently. They may see failure as a temporary obstacle, a learning experience that will help them do better next time. Without the filter of limiting beliefs, they are able to approach life with curiosity and resilience, seeing challenges as part of the journey toward success rather than as a reflection of their inherent worth.

Another significant way that limiting beliefs shape reality is by influencing our self-worth and self-confidence. When we constantly tell ourselves that we're not enough, we start to behave in ways that reflect this belief. We might avoid taking on new challenges, shy away from speaking up in important situations, or settle for less than we deserve in relationships, careers, or personal aspirations. Our actions (or inactions) are shaped by the limiting belief that we don't deserve more or aren't capable of achieving it. Over time, this diminishes our sense of self-worth, leading us to lower our expectations of life and accept far less than what we're truly capable of achieving.

This cycle becomes even more destructive when our limiting beliefs start to influence how we interact with others. In relationships, whether personal or professional, the belief that "I'm not good enough" can cause us to feel inferior or undeserving of respect and love. This may lead to behaviors such as people-pleasing, overcompensating, or tolerating mistreatment. In the workplace, it might manifest as reluctance to advocate for ourselves, whether it's for a raise, a promotion, or recognition for our contributions. The limiting belief convinces us that we're not worthy of more, and so we don't pursue it. Moreover, these beliefs can limit our capacity to see the world's abundance of opportunities. Someone who believes "I'm not capable of success" may be blind to doors opening right in front of them. Even when presented with clear chances for advancement or personal growth, they'll either avoid taking the leap or approach it with so much caution that they fail to seize the opportunity fully. This further perpetuates the cycle of missed chances and confirms their limiting belief that they aren't meant for success.

One particularly dangerous aspect of limiting beliefs is how they shape not just the present but also the future. Every time we allow these beliefs to dictate our actions (or inactions), we are essentially scripting a future that aligns with them. If we repeatedly tell ourselves that we can't succeed, we start to create a reality where that belief holds true. On the other hand, if we challenge and overcome these beliefs, we begin to open ourselves up to new possibilities. The shift in mindset is critical because it redefines what we see as possible and gives us the courage to pursue opportunities that once seemed out of reach.

Limiting beliefs can also distort how we see the success of others. When we operate under the assumption that we aren't capable or deserving of success, we may look at those who are succeeding with resentment or envy. This can lead to the harmful belief that life is unfair, that others are simply more lucky or fortunate, further solidifying the idea that success isn't meant for us. Instead of learning from or being inspired by others, we view their achievements as evidence that we'll never measure up. This only serves to deepen the divide between us and the life we want to live.

Why Awareness Is the Key to Breaking Free

The first step in overcoming limiting beliefs is awareness. We cannot change what we don't acknowledge. By becoming conscious of the beliefs that are holding us back, we can start to challenge and reframe them.

- ❖ **Identify the Belief**: Start by recognizing the belief that's limiting you. What thoughts come up when you think about your goals? Are they empowering or limiting?

- ❖ **Question the Belief**: Once you've identified a limiting belief, ask yourself, "Is this belief really true?" Look for evidence that disproves it. Often, we find that our limiting beliefs are based on fears or past experiences, not objective reality.

- ❖ **Reframe the Belief**: reframe the limiting belief into an empowering one. Instead of thinking, "I'm not capable of succeeding," replace it with, "I am learning and improving with every step I take." By changing the narrative, you change how you approach challenges and opportunities.

Identifying Your Own Limiting Beliefs

Identifying your own limiting beliefs is a critical step toward breaking free from the mental chains that hold you back. Limiting beliefs often operate beneath the surface, subtly influencing your thoughts and actions without your conscious awareness. By engaging in self-reflection and examining your beliefs closely, you can uncover these hidden barriers and start the journey toward personal growth and empowerment. This section will guide you through a self-reflection exercise designed to help you identify your limiting beliefs and understand their impact on your life.

Self-reflection is a powerful tool for personal development. It encourages you to look inward, analyze your thoughts and feelings, and question the narratives that shape your reality. Through self-reflection, you can identify patterns in your thinking and behavior that may be rooted in limiting beliefs. Recognizing these patterns is crucial, as they often dictate your responses to challenges, opportunities, and interpersonal relationships. Understanding how your beliefs affect your life empowers you to challenge and replace them with more constructive and affirming thoughts.

Self-Reflection Exercise: Identifying Your Limiting Beliefs

To begin identifying your limiting beliefs, set aside some quiet time where you can focus on your thoughts without distractions. Grab a journal or a piece of paper and reflect on the following questions. Write down your thoughts and feelings as you respond to each prompt:

1. **What negative thoughts do I frequently have about myself?**

    ❖ Consider the self-talk that runs through your mind on a daily basis. What phrases do you often tell yourself? For instance, do you think, "I'm not smart enough" or "I'll never succeed"? Write down these recurring thoughts.

2. **What situations make me feel uncomfortable or anxious?**

    ❖ Identify scenarios where you feel fear or apprehension. Are there situations, such as public speaking or taking risks, that trigger these feelings? Reflect on how these feelings might be linked to underlying beliefs about your capabilities.

3. **What beliefs do I hold about success and failure?**

   ❖ Analyze your perspective on success and failure. Do you believe that making mistakes equates to failure, or do you view challenges as opportunities for growth? Document your beliefs and consider how they may be limiting your potential.

4. **How do I view my worthiness of happiness and success?**

   ❖ Reflect on whether you believe you deserve happiness and success in your life. Do you feel you have to earn it, or do you believe it is a right for everyone? Write down your feelings and any beliefs that may hinder your pursuit of joy.

5. **What are the stories I tell myself about my past?**

   ❖ Consider how your past experiences shape your current beliefs. Do you often tell yourself that past failures define your future potential? Explore these narratives and how they may be limiting your outlook.

Analyzing Your Responses

After completing the exercise, take time to analyze your responses. Look for recurring themes or specific beliefs that emerge from your reflections. What limiting beliefs stand out the most? Consider how these beliefs have shaped your decisions, actions, and emotional responses throughout your life. This analysis will provide valuable insight into the mental barriers that have held you back.

The Next Steps:

Identifying your limiting beliefs is just the beginning. Once you have a clearer understanding of these beliefs, you can start to challenge and reframe them. Consider asking yourself questions like:

- ❖ Is this belief based on fact or fear?

- ❖ What evidence do I have that contradicts this belief?

- ❖ How would my life change if I let go of this belief?

By actively questioning and reframing your limiting beliefs, you begin to dismantle their power over you. This process takes time and effort, but it is essential for unlocking your potential and creating a life that aligns with your true aspirations. As you work through this journey, remember to practice self-compassion and patience. Growth is a gradual process, and every step you take toward identifying and addressing your limiting beliefs brings you closer to a more fulfilling and empowered life.

CHAPTER TWO

THE NEUROSCIENCE OF BELIEF

Beliefs are more than abstract ideas; they have a tangible effect on our brain and behavior. The neuroscience of beliefs examines the intricate relationship between thoughts, emotions, and neural processes, revealing how beliefs shape our perceptions and influence our actions. By understanding the science behind beliefs, we can gain valuable insights into how they govern our behavior and discover tools to create lasting change. Beliefs are powerful mental constructs that shape how we perceive and interact with the world. They influence our thoughts, emotions, decisions, and behaviors. The neuroscience of belief explores the brain mechanisms and processes that underlie the formation, maintenance, and modification of beliefs. This field examines how the brain creates and sustains beliefs, whether empowering or limiting and their role in guiding our actions.

The Influence of Past Experiences, Emotions, and Environmental Factors

Beliefs don't arise out of nowhere; they are shaped and solidified over time by a combination of past experiences, emotions, and environmental influences. Whether positive or limiting, these deeply rooted beliefs play a significant role in how we perceive and interact with the world. Understanding the origins of beliefs is crucial for recognizing how they influence our present actions and decisions and for creating strategies to challenge and change them when they no longer serve us. Let's explore how each of these elements—past experiences, emotions, and environmental factors—contributes to the formation of beliefs.

The Role of Past Experiences

Our beliefs are often born from the accumulation of experiences over the course of our lives, especially those that are formative, memorable, or emotionally charged. Early childhood experiences, in particular, profoundly impact shaping our beliefs. As children, we absorb information from the world around us, and these early encounters create the foundational framework of our belief systems. For example, a child who receives consistent praise and encouragement is likely to develop a belief that they are capable and deserving of success, while a child who experiences criticism or failure may internalize the belief that they are not good enough or will never succeed.

Positive and negative experiences act like reinforcement mechanisms for belief formation. When we experience success or positive outcomes, our beliefs about our abilities and the world around us tend to be optimistic and empowering. On the other hand, repeated negative experiences, such as failures, rejections, or traumatic events, can lead to the development of limiting beliefs. These experiences become mental "evidence" that we are not capable, not worthy, or that the world is inherently hostile. Over time, these beliefs become ingrained and dictate how we respond to future situations.

Emotions as Drivers of Belief Formation

Emotions play a critical role in how beliefs are formed and reinforced. When an experience is accompanied by a strong emotional response—whether positive or negative—it tends to leave a lasting impression on our minds. This emotional resonance amplifies the significance of the event, making it more likely to shape our beliefs. For example, an experience of public speaking that results in intense embarrassment or shame may lead to the belief that "I'm not good at speaking in front of others." The emotional intensity of the experience strengthens the belief, making it more deeply rooted.

Fear is one of the most powerful emotions that drives the creation of limiting beliefs. When we experience fear—whether it's fear of failure, rejection, or the unknown—we often develop beliefs designed to protect us from future harm. These protective beliefs, though seemingly rational at the time, can become limiting if they prevent us from taking risks or pursuing opportunities. For example, a person who once failed at starting a business might develop the belief that "I'm not cut out for entrepreneurship," not because they lack the skills but because the fear of failure has emotionally reinforced that belief.

On the flip side, positive emotions like joy, pride, and love can also shape empowering beliefs. For instance, someone who has experienced success in a particular area may develop a belief that "I can achieve anything I set my mind to." These emotions fuel the confidence needed to take on challenges and push beyond limitations.

The Influence of Environmental Factors

Beliefs are also shaped by the environment in which we live—our upbringing, culture, family dynamics, and societal influences all contribute to the formation of our belief systems. From a young age, we are exposed to the beliefs of our parents, teachers, and peers, and we often adopt these beliefs without questioning them. For example, suppose a child grows up in a household where education is highly valued. In that case, they will likely develop beliefs that align with the importance of learning and academic achievement. Conversely, suppose a child is raised in an environment where risk-taking is discouraged. In that case, they may develop limiting beliefs about their ability to take risks and step outside their comfort zone.

Cultural norms and societal expectations significantly shape our beliefs about success, relationships, gender roles, and self-worth. For instance, in cultures where perfectionism is highly prized, individuals may develop limiting beliefs centered around the need to be flawless in everything they do. These beliefs can lead to feelings of inadequacy and fear of making mistakes. Similarly, societal pressures around appearance, success, and material wealth can foster beliefs that self-worth is tied to external achievements, leading to a constant pursuit of validation.

Social interactions and relationships also have a profound impact on belief formation. Positive reinforcement from supportive friends or mentors can help solidify empowering beliefs, while negative feedback or criticism from peers, authority figures, or even social media can reinforce limiting beliefs. Over time, these external influences become internalized, shaping our sense of self and what we believe is possible for our lives.

Belief Formation

Beliefs are deeply rooted perceptions that we accept as true, shaped by personal experiences, social conditioning, and cultural influences. From a neurological perspective, belief formation is a complex process that involves multiple regions of the brain working together to interpret, process, and store information.

Understanding how beliefs are formed requires examining the roles of key brain structures, including the prefrontal cortex, hippocampus, amygdala, and the brain's reward pathways.

Key Brain Regions Involved in Belief Formation

1. **Prefrontal Cortex (PFC):**

The prefrontal cortex plays a crucial role in reasoning, decision-making, and goal-directed behavior. It is responsible for filtering and assessing information based on logic and evidence, making it essential for forming rational beliefs. When we encounter new information, the PFC helps us weigh the facts, evaluate the reliability of the source, and ultimately decide what we accept as true or false. This process allows for the formation of beliefs based on conscious thought and reasoned judgment.

The PFC also helps us update our beliefs when we are presented with new information that contradicts our existing views. This capacity to change or adapt beliefs is a key feature of cognitive flexibility, which enables individuals to grow and evolve over time.

2. **Hippocampus:**

The hippocampus is responsible for memory formation and retrieval, making it a vital component in the process of belief formation. Past experiences often shape beliefs, and the hippocampus helps store these experiences as memories. When we encounter new situations or information, the hippocampus integrates these new experiences with existing knowledge. This process allows us to form beliefs based on immediate experiences and the accumulation of past events.

For example, if someone repeatedly experiences success in certain endeavors, the hippocampus stores these memories, which in turn may reinforce a belief in their ability to succeed. Conversely, negative past experiences can solidify beliefs of self-doubt or fear of failure.

3. Amygdala:

The amygdala is primarily involved in emotional processing and plays a significant role in how emotions influence our beliefs. Strong emotions, particularly those related to fear or pleasure, can profoundly shape the beliefs we hold. The amygdala helps encode these emotionally charged experiences, making beliefs associated with intense emotions particularly resilient.

For instance, beliefs formed in response to fear, such as a belief that a particular activity is dangerous, may be more difficult to change, even when presented with evidence to the contrary. The emotional power of the amygdala often causes such beliefs to be stored more vividly and remain resistant to logic or rationality.

4. Limbic System and Reward Pathways:

The limbic system, of which the amygdala is a part, interacts with the brain's reward pathways to reinforce certain beliefs over time. The reward system, involving neurotransmitters like dopamine, plays a critical role in reinforcing beliefs by associating them with feelings of reward or pleasure. When an action or thought leads to a positive outcome (e.g., praise, validation, or success), the brain releases dopamine, reinforcing the belief that the action or thought is valid or beneficial.

This neurological feedback loop explains why we tend to hold onto beliefs that have led to positive outcomes in the past. For instance, if someone repeatedly receives social validation for a particular opinion, the brain's reward system will strengthen that belief. Conversely, beliefs associated with negative feedback, such as social rejection or failure, may become linked with fear or doubt, reinforcing limiting or negative beliefs.

How Beliefs Are Formed and Reinforced

Beliefs are formed through experiences, learning, and social influences. The brain organizes information from the environment and encodes it into beliefs through memory, emotion, and reasoning.

When we encounter new information, our brain processes it using cognitive (logical) and emotional (affective) systems. Experiences, especially those emotionally charged, leave lasting impressions in the brain, contributing to the development of beliefs. These beliefs are further reinforced through repeated experiences, whether they result in positive outcomes (reinforcing belief in success) or negative consequences (reinforcing self-doubt or fear).

The prefrontal cortex helps us assess whether information aligns with existing beliefs or challenges them. The hippocampus integrates new knowledge with stored memories. At the same time, the amygdala ensures that emotionally significant events, especially those associated with strong feelings like fear or joy, are stored vividly and influence future decisions. The brain's reward pathways work to solidify beliefs that lead to rewarding or successful outcomes, making them more challenging to change.

The Role of the Prefrontal Cortex in Decision-Making and Belief Formation

The prefrontal cortex (PFC) is crucial for higher cognitive functions like decision-making, self-control, and problem-solving. It plays a key role in belief formation by processing past experiences, emotions, and environmental factors. This area helps us interpret reality, guiding our responses based on what we believe about ourselves and the world.

Prefrontal Cortex and Decision-Making

Decision-making is one of the prefrontal cortex's most important functions, intricately connected to forming and reinforcing beliefs. Every decision we make is filtered through our existing beliefs, which serve as cognitive shortcuts, helping the brain process information more efficiently. If, for instance, we hold a belief that we are bad at public speaking, the prefrontal cortex may prompt us to avoid opportunities for public speaking, reinforcing the limiting belief. A key aspect of decision-making is evaluating whether a belief aligns with evidence and rational thought. The prefrontal cortex allows us to assess whether a particular belief serves or holds us back. For example, someone who believes they are incapable of learning new skills might, through deliberate reflection facilitated by the prefrontal cortex, begin to question this belief, especially

Drawing from Past Experiences

Belief formation is closely linked to the brain's ability to draw on past experiences, and the prefrontal cortex plays a central role in this process. When we encounter a new situation, the prefrontal cortex processes it by recalling similar past experiences. These past experiences create mental frameworks or schemas that help us interpret and respond to new events. Over time, these interpretations solidify into beliefs.

For instance, if someone has repeatedly experienced failure when attempting to learn new skills, the prefrontal cortex may reinforce the belief that "I am bad at learning." This belief becomes ingrained as the brain continuously references past failures whenever a similar situation arises. Each time the individual is faced with a new learning challenge, the prefrontal cortex consults the "evidence" of past failures, strengthening the limiting belief.

On the other hand, empowering beliefs can also be formed through the same process. If an individual consistently receives positive feedback and experiences success in their endeavors, the prefrontal cortex builds a belief system that supports self-efficacy and confidence. The brain uses past experiences as a reference point for future decisions, reinforcing positive beliefs and encouraging a growth mindset.

The Role of Emotions in Belief Formation and the Prefrontal Cortex

Emotions are another significant factor in how beliefs are formed and maintained, and the prefrontal cortex helps regulate our emotional responses to different situations. Strong emotional experiences, particularly those tied to fear, success, failure, or joy, influence our beliefs. The prefrontal cortex interacts with other brain regions, such as the amygdala, which processes emotions like fear and pleasure, to assess and regulate emotional reactions.

When a highly emotional event occurs, such as a traumatic failure or a moment of public humiliation, the prefrontal cortex processes the emotional intensity and encodes it into memory. This emotional imprint makes the experience particularly memorable and may lead to the formation of a limiting belief. For instance, a person who was ridiculed during a public speaking engagement may develop a deeply held belief that they are bad at public speaking, a belief that is reinforced by the emotional trauma of the experience.

Conversely, the prefrontal cortex also processes positive emotions and experiences, allowing for the formation of empowering beliefs. For example, an individual who wins an award for their work might form the belief that they are talented or capable, with the emotional reward of success reinforcing this belief over time.

Environmental Factors and the Role of the Prefrontal Cortex in Belief Formation

The environment in which we live plays a significant role in shaping our beliefs, and the prefrontal cortex helps us navigate and interpret these environmental influences. From childhood, we are exposed to a range of environmental factors, including family dynamics, cultural values, societal expectations, and peer influences. These factors contribute to the development of our belief systems.

The prefrontal cortex allows us to evaluate and internalize these environmental inputs. For example, suppose someone grows up in a family that highly values academic achievement. In that case, the prefrontal cortex will help integrate this environmental expectation into the individual's belief system, potentially leading to the belief that academic success is a primary measure of worth. Whether empowering or limiting, this belief will influence future decisions about education, career, and personal development.

Moreover, the prefrontal cortex helps us adapt our beliefs based on changing environmental circumstances. The prefrontal cortex evaluates whether existing beliefs still serve us as we encounter new information or move into different social contexts. For instance, someone who moves from a conservative, risk-averse environment to a more innovative, entrepreneurial setting may begin to challenge limiting beliefs about risk-taking spurred by new environmental cues.

The Limbic System and Emotional Ties to Belief

The limbic system is a complex set of structures in the brain that plays a pivotal role in regulating emotions, memory, and motivation. This system is crucial in shaping and reinforcing our beliefs, as it directly connects emotional experiences with the cognitive processes that lead to belief formation.

Emotional Influence on Beliefs

Emotions are powerful drivers of our beliefs. When we experience an event that elicits a strong emotional response, the limbic system encodes that emotion alongside the experience. For instance, a positive emotional experience, such as receiving praise, can foster a belief in one's abilities and worth. Conversely, negative emotional experiences, like criticism or failure, can lead to limiting beliefs, such as "I'm not capable" or "I will always fail." These beliefs can become ingrained, influencing how we interpret future situations and respond to challenges.

Reinforcement of Beliefs Through Emotional Reactions

The limbic system continually reinforces beliefs through emotional reactions. When an emotional experience aligns with an existing belief, it strengthens that belief. For instance, if someone believes they are unworthy and repeatedly faces rejection, the emotional pain from those experiences solidifies the belief. This cycle can trap individuals in a negative reinforcement loop, making breaking free from limiting beliefs difficult.

The Role of Memory in Belief Formation

The limbic system's connection to memory is critical in belief formation. Emotional memories tend to be more vivid and impactful, making them more likely to influence future beliefs. When individuals recall emotional events, they often remember not just the event itself but the accompanying feelings, which shapes their understanding of similar situations in the future. This emotional memory can solidify beliefs, making them feel more real and valid, even if they are based on limited or skewed experiences.

Understanding the limbic system's role in belief formation highlights the importance of addressing emotional ties when working to change beliefs. By recognizing how emotions shape our perceptions, individuals can begin to challenge and reframe limiting beliefs. Techniques such as mindfulness, cognitive restructuring, and emotional processing can help individuals dissociate negative emotional experiences from their beliefs, allowing for the development of a more empowering mindset.

Neuroplasticity and Belief Flexibility

Neuroplasticity, the brain's remarkable ability to reorganize itself by forming new neural connections, plays a vital role in belief flexibility. This phenomenon is fundamental to personal growth, as it enables individuals to adapt their beliefs in response to new experiences, information, and insights. Understanding neuroplasticity provides a framework for recognizing how we can challenge and change limiting beliefs that may have previously felt immutable.

Neuroplasticity refers to the brain's capacity to change and adapt throughout a person's life. This capability allows the brain to reorganize itself by creating new neural pathways and connections in response to learning, experience, or injury. Neuroplasticity occurs at various levels, from cellular changes (involving neurons and synapses) to large-scale changes in brain structure and function. It is most pronounced during childhood but continues throughout adulthood, enabling ongoing learning and adaptation.

The Process of Changing Beliefs

Beliefs are not fixed; they can be modified through experience and reflection. Neuroplasticity allows for this change through several processes:

- **Learning New Information:** When individuals encounter new ideas or evidence that contradict their existing beliefs, the brain can reorganize to accommodate this new information. For example, learning about successful individuals who overcame similar challenges can shift a belief from "I can't succeed" to "If they can do it, so can I." This cognitive shift often requires repeated exposure to the new information, allowing the brain to solidify new pathways that support the revised belief.

- **Challenging Existing Beliefs:** Engaging in critical thinking and self-reflection can challenge deeply held beliefs. When individuals actively question the validity of their beliefs, they stimulate neuroplasticity by promoting the formation of alternative perspectives. For instance, someone who believes they are not creative may begin experimenting with artistic endeavors, leading to new experiences that reshape their self-perception.

- **Mindfulness and Emotional Regulation:** Mindfulness practices can foster neuroplasticity by encouraging emotional regulation and enhancing self-awareness. By practicing mindfulness, individuals can observe their thoughts and beliefs without judgment, allowing for a more objective analysis of their validity. This practice can create a space for new beliefs to emerge and take root in the brain.

The Impact of New Experiences

Exposure to new experiences plays a critical role in reshaping beliefs. As the brain encounters novel situations, it collects data that can challenge preconceived notions and foster flexibility. For instance:

- **Diverse Interactions:** Engaging with people from different backgrounds and perspectives can broaden one's understanding of the world. These interactions can challenge stereotypes and limiting beliefs, promoting empathy and openness. For example, someone who holds a belief that a specific group is untrustworthy may change this view after forming genuine connections with individuals from that group.

- **Travel and Cultural Exposure:** Traveling to new places exposes individuals to different cultures, ideas, and ways of life. This exposure can challenge entrenched beliefs and encourage a more nuanced understanding of diverse perspectives. For instance, experiencing a culture that values community over individualism may reshape beliefs about success and fulfillment.

- **Education and Continuous Learning:** Pursuing lifelong learning can foster neuroplasticity. New knowledge can challenge outdated beliefs, prompting individuals to reassess their understanding of themselves and the world. Engaging in courses or workshops that focus on personal development can provide tools and strategies to cultivate a growth mindset.

Changing Beliefs Through Brain Rewiring

Changing deeply ingrained beliefs is not just a matter of willpower or positive thinking; it involves a fundamental brain rewiring process. This process taps into the brain's neuroplasticity, allowing individuals to replace negative thought patterns with empowering beliefs. By understanding how to reshape our thinking intentionally, we can break free from limiting beliefs and foster a more positive and fulfilling mindset.

Neural pathways are the connections between neurons that facilitate communication within the brain. When we engage in repetitive thoughts or behaviors, these pathways strengthen, making those thoughts or behaviors easier to access in the future. Conversely, the associated neural pathways can weaken when we stop engaging in specific thought patterns. This phenomenon is known as "use it or lose it," meaning that the pathways we reinforce become more pronounced while those we neglect diminish.

The Process of Rewiring the Brain

The brain is an incredibly adaptable organ, capable of change and growth throughout a person's life. This phenomenon, known as neuroplasticity, is the foundation for rewiring the brain, allowing individuals to alter their thoughts, beliefs, and behaviors. Understanding this process is crucial for anyone seeking to change limiting beliefs and foster a more positive mindset. The journey of rewiring the brain involves several interconnected steps, including awareness, intention, practice, and reinforcement.

1. **Awareness and Recognition**

   The first step in the process of rewiring the brain is developing awareness of existing thoughts and beliefs. This involves recognizing the limiting beliefs that have shaped one's mindset and behaviors. Often, these beliefs operate unconsciously, affecting decisions and emotional responses without conscious thought.

   Individuals can engage in self-reflection practices, such as journaling or mindfulness meditation, to cultivate awareness. These practices help identify negative thought patterns and emotional triggers that reinforce limiting beliefs. For instance, someone might realize they frequently think, "I am not good enough," in situations requiring self-confidence. Acknowledging these thoughts is essential, as it lays the groundwork for meaningful change.

2. **Challenging Negative Thoughts**

   Once awareness is established, the next step is to challenge the negative thoughts and beliefs identified. This process involves critically examining the validity of these beliefs and seeking evidence that contradicts them. Individuals can ask themselves reflective questions, such as:

   - What evidence do I have that supports or contradicts this belief?

   - How would I perceive this situation if I held a more empowering belief?

- What would I tell a friend facing similar thoughts?

By questioning the validity of limiting beliefs, individuals can weaken their hold and create space for new, more empowering beliefs to emerge.

3. **Intentional Thought Patterns**

To rewire the brain, actively replacing negative thoughts with intentional, positive affirmations is essential. This step involves consciously choosing to think positively and reinforce new beliefs. Positive affirmations serve as powerful tools for reshaping thought patterns, as they encourage individuals to visualize themselves achieving their goals or embodying desired traits.

For example, someone who struggles with self-doubt might repeat affirmations such as "I am capable" or "I deserve success." By consistently practicing these affirmations, individuals gradually strengthen the neural pathways associated with positive beliefs. The key is to repeat these affirmations regularly, allowing them to become ingrained in the mind.

4. **Visualization and Mental Rehearsal**

Visualization is another effective technique in the rewiring process. This practice involves mentally picturing oneself successfully achieving goals or embodying new beliefs. Visualization activates the same neural pathways as real-life experiences, making it a powerful tool for belief change.

For example, if someone wants to become a confident public speaker, they can visualize themselves speaking in front of an audience, feeling calm and self-assured. This mental rehearsal reinforces the desired belief and prepares the brain for real-life scenarios, increasing confidence and reducing anxiety.

5. **Behavioral Experiments and Incremental Challenges**

Engaging in behavioral experiments is crucial for reinforcing new beliefs and creating lasting change. This involves stepping out of one's comfort zone and taking small, incremental risks that challenge negative beliefs. By actively engaging in experiences contradicting limiting beliefs, individuals can gather evidence supporting their new, empowering mindset.

For instance, someone who believes they are not sociable can set a goal to initiate conversations with strangers or attend social events. Each successful interaction reinforces the belief that they can connect with others, gradually rewiring their brain to support this newfound identity.

6. **Building a Supportive Environment**

The environment plays a significant role in the brain rewiring process. Surrounding oneself with supportive people and positive influences can foster belief change. Engaging with mentors, friends, or communities that encourage personal growth can provide motivation and reinforcement for new beliefs.

Creating a physical space reflecting positive beliefs can enhance the rewiring process. For example, displaying inspirational quotes, images, or reminders of past achievements can continuously affirm new beliefs, reinforcing the journey toward personal growth.

7. **Persistence and Practice**

Rewiring the brain is not a one-time event but a continuous process that requires persistence and consistent practice. Just as negative beliefs take time to develop, positive beliefs will also take time to strengthen. Individuals must commit to their journey of self-discovery and growth, understanding that setbacks and challenges are a natural part of the process.

Regularly revisiting self-reflection practices, affirmations, and behavioral experiments will reinforce the new neural pathways formed during rewiring. Over time, these pathways will become stronger, leading to lasting changes in beliefs and behaviors.

The role of mindfulness, meditation, and cognitive-behavioral techniques in changing beliefs

Mindfulness, meditation, and cognitive-behavioral techniques are interconnected practices that play a crucial role in changing beliefs, particularly limiting or detrimental ones. **Mindfulness** involves:

- Cultivating an awareness of the present moment.

- Allowing individuals to observe their thoughts and emotions.

- Bodily sensations without judgment.

This practice is fundamental for recognizing limiting beliefs as they arise. By becoming more aware of automatic thought patterns, individuals can identify negative self-talk and irrational beliefs that influence their decisions and behaviors. Mindfulness helps create a mental space between stimulus and response, allowing individuals to pause and choose how to react rather than being governed by ingrained beliefs. This awareness is the first step in challenging and changing those beliefs, as it empowers individuals to engage with their thought processes consciously.

Meditation, especially techniques focused on visualization and positive affirmations, can significantly enhance the process of belief change. By dedicating time to visualize desired outcomes or repeating affirmations that reinforce new, empowering beliefs, individuals can train their brains to adopt these new narratives. For example, a person who struggles with feelings of inadequacy can meditate on affirmations like "I am enough" or visualize themselves succeeding in areas they previously thought were unattainable. Over time, such practices can lead to physiological changes in the brain, promoting neuroplasticity, which is the brain's ability to reorganize itself by forming new neural connections. As individuals repeatedly engage in these meditative practices, they effectively create new pathways that support healthier beliefs, gradually diminishing the power of limiting beliefs.

Cognitive-behavioral techniques complement mindfulness and meditation by providing structured methods for identifying and reframing limiting beliefs. Cognitive-behavioral therapy (CBT) encourages individuals to challenge negative thoughts by examining evidence, considering alternative perspectives, and identifying cognitive distortions. For instance, someone who believes they cannot pursue a new career might be prompted to list past accomplishments, skills, and the positive feedback they have received from others. This reframing process helps to undermine the validity of limiting beliefs and encourages the adoption of a more balanced, realistic perspective. By integrating mindfulness, meditation, and cognitive-behavioral techniques, individuals can cultivate a holistic approach to belief change that promotes emotional resilience, empowers personal growth, and fosters a greater sense of self-efficacy.

Practical Strategies for Harnessing the Neuroscience of Belief

Harnessing the power of belief through an understanding of neuroscience offers practical strategies for personal transformation. By applying brain insights, individuals can develop techniques to reshape their beliefs and foster a growth mindset. Here are several practical strategies grounded in the neuroscience of belief:

Positive Affirmations and Self-Talk

One effective strategy for changing beliefs is using positive affirmations and constructive self-talk. Repeating affirmations—statements that reflect the beliefs you want to adopt—can help rewire your brain to accept these new beliefs as truth. For instance, if you struggle with feelings of unworthiness, affirmations like "I am capable and deserving of success" can replace negative self-talk. Neuroscience shows that consistently repeating positive affirmations activates the brain's reward centers, reinforcing a sense of self-efficacy and boosting motivation. Over time, these affirmations can help create new neural pathways that support positive beliefs and diminish the impact of limiting ones.

Mindfulness Practices

Incorporating mindfulness practices into daily routines can significantly enhance self-awareness and belief transformation. Mindfulness encourages individuals to observe their thoughts and feelings without judgment, allowing them to identify limiting beliefs as they arise. Techniques such as mindful breathing, body scans, or mindful observation can ground individuals in the present moment, helping them detach from negative thought patterns. This practice can facilitate a greater understanding of how emotions influence beliefs, enabling individuals to challenge and reframe those beliefs more effectively. Mindfulness promotes neuroplasticity by reducing stress and increasing the brain's ability to adapt and form new connections.

Cognitive Restructuring

Cognitive restructuring is a core component of cognitive-behavioral techniques that involves identifying and challenging negative thoughts and beliefs. To implement this strategy, individuals can keep a journal to track their limiting beliefs and the circumstances that trigger them. Individuals can reframe their perspectives by examining these beliefs critically—questioning their validity and exploring evidence to the contrary. For example, someone who believes they are not skilled enough to pursue a new job can list their accomplishments, skills, and experiences that support their capability. This process helps weaken the grip of limiting beliefs and enhances self-awareness and emotional resilience.

Visualization Techniques

Visualization is a powerful tool for harnessing the brain's potential to create new beliefs. By vividly imagining desired outcomes or successful scenarios, individuals can train their brains to recognize them as achievable. Visualization can be practiced in various ways, such as visualizing a successful presentation or imagining oneself confidently tackling a challenging task. This technique taps into the brain's neural pathways, reinforcing a sense of possibility and readiness. Regular visualization practice can lead to brain structure and function changes, enhancing motivation and belief in one's abilities.

Engaging in New Experiences

Engaging in new experiences and challenges can foster the development of new beliefs by providing opportunities for learning and growth. Whether trying a new hobby, taking a class, or stepping outside one's comfort zone, these experiences can help individuals gather evidence against their limiting beliefs. By overcoming challenges and succeeding in new endeavors, individuals can create positive reinforcement for their capabilities. Neuroscience shows that exposure to new experiences can stimulate the brain's plasticity, encouraging the formation of new neural connections and pathways that support a more expansive belief system.

By utilizing these practical strategies rooted in the neuroscience of belief, individuals can actively work towards changing their limiting beliefs and fostering a more empowering mindset. The brain's remarkable capacity for change offers hope and potential for personal transformation, allowing individuals to break free from the constraints of their past and embrace a future filled with possibilities. As you integrate these strategies into your daily life, remember that belief is not static; it is a dynamic force that can be shaped and reshaped through intentional effort and practice.

Limiting beliefs are invisible barriers that prevent us from reaching our full potential and achieving our goals. These self-imposed limitations restrict our abilities, choices, and opportunities, often without us realizing it. Identifying these beliefs is the first step to breaking free from them and beginning a journey of growth and empowerment.

What Are Limiting Beliefs?

Limiting beliefs are persistent thoughts that we accept as true without questioning their validity. They shape our identity, influence our behavior, and determine what we believe is possible. These beliefs can manifest in various ways, including self-doubt, fear, and negative self-talk. They often stem from early experiences, cultural conditioning, or the messages we receive from family, peers, and society. For instance, a child who hears repeatedly that they are not good at math may grow into an adult who shies away from any task involving numbers, regardless of their actual abilities.

A common limiting belief is the fear of failure. This belief makes us think that making mistakes is a reflection of our worth or abilities. As a result, we may avoid challenges or opportunities that could lead to growth, choosing instead to remain in our comfort zones. Fear of failure stifles innovation, creativity, and progress, thereby limiting our ability to learn and grow. In a professional context, for instance, someone may decline a job opportunity or promotion because they fear they won't be able to meet expectations, even if they possess the skills required. This self-sabotage can perpetuate a cycle of underachievement, reinforcing the original limiting belief.

Another prevalent limiting belief is the fear of judgment. This belief leads us to prioritize the opinions of others over our own needs and desires. We may fear rejection, criticism, or disapproval, leading us to conform to societal expectations instead of pursuing our true path. Fear of judgment can stifle our self-expression, creativity, and individuality, preventing us from being authentic. For example, an aspiring artist may choose a more conventional career path because they fear that their art will not be appreciated or that they will face ridicule. By allowing the fear of judgment to dictate their choices, they limit their potential for fulfillment and self-actualization.

Common Examples of Limiting Beliefs

Limiting beliefs can vary widely among individuals, but certain themes tend to emerge frequently. Here are some common examples that many people may encounter at different stages in their lives:

- **Fear of Failure**: This belief manifests as a pervasive fear that making mistakes or experiencing setbacks reflects poorly on one's abilities or worth. Individuals may think, "If I fail, it means I'm not capable," leading them to avoid challenges and opportunities for growth. This fear can stifle creativity, innovation, and personal development.

- **Not Good Enough**: Many people struggle with the belief that they are inadequate or not deserving of success and happiness. Phrases like "I'm not smart enough" or "I don't have the right skills" often accompany this belief. This mindset can prevent individuals from pursuing their goals, leading to missed opportunities and unfulfilled potential.

- **Fear of Judgment**: This belief centers around the idea that others will judge or criticize us for our choices, appearance, or abilities. Thoughts such as "What will people think?" can inhibit self-expression and discourage individuals from pursuing their passions, leading them to conform to societal norms instead of embracing their authentic selves.

- **Imposter Syndrome**: Imposter syndrome is a common phenomenon where individuals believe they are frauds despite their accomplishments. They may feel that their success is due to luck or external factors rather than their skills or hard work. This belief can lead to chronic self-doubt and anxiety, preventing individuals from fully embracing their achievements.

- **Fear of Change**: Many people resist change, believing that stepping out of their comfort zone will lead to negative consequences. They might think, "Things will only worsen if I try something new." This belief can limit personal growth and hinder the exploration of new opportunities.

- **Deservingness**: Some individuals hold the belief that they do not deserve love, happiness, or success. They may think, "I'm not worthy of a good relationship," or "I don't deserve happiness." This mindset can lead to self-sabotaging behaviors, such as pushing away supportive relationships or avoiding experiences that bring joy.

- **Age-Related Beliefs**: Many people believe they are too old or young to pursue certain goals. Phrases like "I missed my chance" or "I'm too young to be taken seriously" can prevent individuals from taking action, regardless of their actual capabilities or opportunities.

- **Financial Limitations**: Beliefs about money, such as "I'll never be wealthy" or "Money is the root of all evil," can restrict financial growth and personal fulfillment. These beliefs can lead to poor financial decisions and a reluctance to pursue wealth-building opportunities.

- **Beliefs about Relationships**: Individuals may hold limiting beliefs regarding their ability to maintain healthy relationships. Thoughts like "I always mess up relationships" or "Love is not meant for me" can hinder their willingness to seek or invest in meaningful connections.

The Origins of Limiting Beliefs

Limiting beliefs are not inherent to our nature; they are learned and developed over time through various influences and experiences. These beliefs often stem from a combination of personal experiences, social conditioning, and cultural influences. From childhood, we absorb messages from our environment and internalize beliefs about ourselves and the world around us. Understanding the origins of these limiting beliefs is essential for breaking free from their constraints and fostering a more empowering mindset.

❖ Personal Experiences

Our upbringing plays a crucial role in shaping our beliefs, particularly during the formative years of childhood. The experiences we have—both positive and negative—leave lasting marks on our psyche. For instance, a child who struggles academically might develop the belief that they are unintelligent or incapable of success. This self-perception can become ingrained over time, leading to a cycle of underachievement as the child avoids challenges that could contradict this belief. Similarly, experiences of failure, rejection, or criticism can foster a sense of inadequacy. A child who receives harsh feedback from teachers or peers may internalize these messages, shaping their self-esteem and influencing their willingness to take risks later in life.

Traumatic experiences can create even more profound limiting beliefs. Individuals who have faced abuse, neglect, or significant trauma often carry beliefs of unworthiness or lack of control into adulthood. These deeply rooted beliefs can affect self-esteem, relationships, and decision-making processes. For instance, a person who has experienced emotional abuse may struggle with trusting others or believing they are deserving of healthy relationships. Overcoming these limiting beliefs typically requires a process of healing and reframing past experiences to foster a more empowering perspective. Therapeutic interventions, support networks, and self-reflection can be instrumental in this journey, enabling individuals to reinterpret their narratives and reclaim their sense of agency.

❖ Social Conditioning

Social conditioning refers to the influence of societal norms, values, and expectations on our beliefs and behaviors. Family dynamics and expectations significantly impact our perceptions of what is achievable in life. For example, children raised in environments that prioritize academic success may internalize the belief that their worth is directly tied to their achievements. This belief can lead to immense pressure to perform, which in turn stifles creativity and exploration outside of academic pursuits. The fear of disappointing family members can create a cycle of stress and anxiety, further entrenching the belief that one's value is dependent on external validation.

Peer interactions also play a critical role in shaping our beliefs. The desire for conformity and acceptance can lead individuals to adopt beliefs that align with group norms, sometimes at the expense of their own values or individuality. For instance, a teenager may feel pressured to engage in behaviors that conflict with their personal beliefs to fit in with a social group. Overcoming social conditioning involves cultivating self-awareness and embracing authenticity, allowing individuals to navigate their paths without succumbing to the expectations of others. It requires the courage to assert one's identity and values, even when they diverge from the dominant narratives in one's environment.

❖ Cultural Influences

Cultural influences significantly shape our beliefs about gender roles, success, and identity. Societal expectations around appearance, behavior, and achievement influence how we perceive ourselves and what we believe is possible. Cultural messages regarding what is valuable or acceptable can limit our beliefs about our strengths and abilities. For example, cultural stereotypes about gender roles may lead individuals to believe that certain careers or opportunities are inaccessible based on their gender. A girl may be discouraged from pursuing a career in science or technology due to the belief that these fields are male-dominated, while a boy may feel pressure to conform to traditional masculine roles that deter him from exploring interests in the arts.

Challenging these cultural influences involves recognizing and questioning societal norms, embracing diversity, and promoting equality. This process requires individual reflection and collective action to dismantle stereotypes and broaden the scope of what is deemed acceptable or achievable. Engaging in conversations about gender equality, representation, and cultural diversity can empower individuals to redefine their beliefs and create a more inclusive narrative that celebrates the unique contributions of all people. By doing so, we can foster an environment that nurtures growth, creativity, and authenticity, enabling everyone to pursue their passions without the constraints of limiting beliefs.

Understanding the origins of limiting beliefs provides critical insight into how we can identify and dismantle these barriers. By examining our personal experiences, social conditioning, and cultural influences, we can begin to unravel the narratives that have shaped our identities and perceptions. This awareness is the first step toward reclaiming our potential and embracing a more empowering belief system that fosters growth, resilience, and self-actualization.

The Process of Identifying Limiting Beliefs

Identifying limiting beliefs requires introspection and self-awareness. Here are some practical steps to help you uncover your own limiting beliefs:

- **Self-Reflection Journaling**: Set aside time to write about your thoughts, feelings, and behaviors. Ask yourself questions such as, "What do I believe about myself?" or "What fears hold me back from pursuing my goals?" This process can help illuminate patterns in your thinking and reveal underlying beliefs.

- **Mindfulness Practices**: Mindfulness can help you become aware of your thoughts and feelings in the present moment. By practicing mindfulness, you can observe your internal dialogue and notice when limiting beliefs arise. This awareness is crucial for challenging and changing those beliefs.

- **Seek Feedback**: Sometimes, our beliefs are so ingrained that we struggle to see them ourselves. Asking trusted friends, family members, or mentors for their perspective on your strengths and weaknesses can provide valuable insights into your limiting beliefs.

- **Challenge Negative Self-Talk**: Pay attention to the language you use when thinking or speaking about yourself. Notice any recurring phrases or themes that indicate limiting beliefs, such as "I'm not good enough" or "I can't do this." When you identify these patterns, consciously reframe them with more positive and empowering affirmations.

- **Visualize Your Goals**: Visualization techniques can help you see beyond your current limitations. Picture yourself achieving your goals and consider the beliefs that may be holding you back. This exercise can create a contrast between your aspirations and your current mindset, highlighting the beliefs that need to change.

The Importance of Challenging Limiting Beliefs

Once you have identified your limiting beliefs, the next step is to challenge them. Understanding that these beliefs are not truths but rather subjective perceptions is essential for growth. You can start by questioning the validity of each belief:

- Where did this belief come from?

- Is there evidence that contradicts this belief?

- What would I say to a friend who held this belief?

By systematically examining the origins and implications of your limiting beliefs, you can begin to dismantle their power over your life. Remember, the goal is not to eradicate all beliefs but to cultivate a mindset that embraces possibility and growth.

The Impact of Limiting Beliefs

Limiting beliefs can profoundly impact our lives, including self-esteem, relationships, careers, and overall well-being. These beliefs create mental frameworks that shape our identities and perspectives, often leading to self-sabotage and missed opportunities. Understanding the ramifications of limiting beliefs is crucial to recognizing their hold on our lives and taking steps to overcome them.

1. **Self-Esteem and Self-Worth:** Limiting beliefs fundamentally undermine our self-esteem and self-worth, fostering a climate of self-doubt and hesitation. When we internalize negative beliefs about ourselves, we see the world through a distorted lens, emphasizing inadequacies rather than strengths. This internal dialogue, characterized by negative self-talk, reinforces limiting beliefs, leading to a cycle of insecurity. For instance, someone who believes they are unworthy of

love may constantly question their attractiveness or value, convincing themselves that they do not deserve healthy relationships. This internal struggle can prevent them from pursuing fulfilling experiences or connections, further entrenching their feelings of inadequacy.

The cycle of negative self-talk and self-doubt can manifest in various ways, often leading to missed opportunities for growth and success. We inadvertently sabotage our potential when we hesitate to put ourselves forward, whether for a promotion, a new relationship, or any opportunity that requires stepping out of our comfort zone. Overcoming these deeply ingrained beliefs requires a multifaceted approach that includes cultivating self-compassion, actively challenging negative self-talk, and embracing self-acceptance. By acknowledging our intrinsic worth and recognizing that everyone has strengths and weaknesses, we can begin to dismantle these limiting beliefs and build a healthier self-image.

2. **Relationships and Social Interactions:** Limiting beliefs profoundly affect our relationships and social interactions, dictating how we connect with others. Beliefs about our worth, desirability, and ability to form bonds can lead to significant barriers to establishing meaningful connections. For instance, someone who believes they are unworthy of love may find it challenging to trust others or to open up emotionally, resulting in strained relationships. Fear of rejection or judgment often leads to social anxiety, making individuals retreat into isolation rather than actively engaging with their communities.

In this context, limiting beliefs can create a self-fulfilling prophecy. The more we believe we are unworthy of love or acceptance, the more likely we are to behave in ways that reinforce these beliefs, such as avoiding social situations or sabotaging relationships before they can develop. Challenging these beliefs is critical for developing trust and vulnerability in our interactions. By fostering effective communication skills and opening ourselves up to authentic connections, we can dismantle the barriers erected by limiting beliefs and cultivate supportive and enriching relationships. This process involves personal reflection and seeking environments that encourage growth and acceptance.

3. **Career and Achievement:** Limiting beliefs significantly hinders our career growth and achievement, often manifesting as fears of inadequacy or imposter syndrome. Beliefs about our abilities or potential can prevent us from pursuing opportunities that could lead to advancement or fulfillment. For example, someone may possess the necessary skills and expertise but still hesitate to apply for a promotion because they believe they are not "cut out" for leadership roles. This fear can lead to procrastination, avoidance, and ultimately self-sabotage, as individuals convince themselves they will fail or are not worthy of success.

Identifying Your Own Limiting Beliefs

Identifying your own limiting beliefs is a critical step toward breaking free from the mental chains that hold you back. Limiting beliefs often operate beneath the surface, subtly influencing your thoughts and actions without your conscious awareness. By engaging in self-reflection and examining your beliefs closely, you can uncover these hidden barriers and start the journey toward personal growth and empowerment. This section will guide you through a self-reflection exercise designed to help you identify your limiting beliefs and understand their impact on your life.

Self-reflection is a powerful tool for personal development. It encourages you to look inward, analyze your thoughts and feelings, and question the narratives that shape your reality. Through self-reflection, you can identify patterns in your thinking and behavior that may be rooted in limiting beliefs. Recognizing these patterns is crucial, as they often dictate your responses to challenges, opportunities, and interpersonal relationships. Understanding how your beliefs affect your life empowers you to challenge and replace them with more constructive and affirming thoughts.

Self-Reflection Exercise: Identifying Your Limiting Beliefs

To begin identifying your limiting beliefs, set aside some quiet time where you can focus on your thoughts without distractions. Grab a journal or a piece of paper and reflect on the following questions. Write down your thoughts and feelings as you respond to each prompt:

1. **What negative thoughts do I frequently have about myself?**

   ❖ Consider the self-talk that runs through your mind on a daily basis. What phrases do you often tell yourself? For instance, do you think, "I'm not smart enough" or "I'll never succeed"? Write down these recurring thoughts.

2. **What situations make me feel uncomfortable or anxious?**

   ❖ Identify scenarios where you feel fear or apprehension. Are there situations, such as public speaking or taking risks, that trigger these feelings? Reflect on how these feelings might be linked to underlying beliefs about your capabilities.

3. **What beliefs do I hold about success and failure?**

   ❖ Analyze your perspective on success and failure. Do you believe that making mistakes equates to failure, or do you view challenges as opportunities for growth? Document your beliefs and consider how they may be limiting your potential.

4. **How do I view my worthiness of happiness and success?**

   ❖ Reflect on whether you believe you deserve happiness and success in your life. Do you feel you have to earn it, or do you believe it is a right for everyone? Write down your feelings and any beliefs that may hinder your pursuit of joy.

5. **What are the stories I tell myself about my past?**

❖ Consider how your past experiences shape your current beliefs. Do you often tell yourself that past failures define your future potential? Explore these narratives and how they may be limiting your outlook.

Analyzing Your Responses

After completing the exercise, take time to analyze your responses. Look for recurring themes or specific beliefs that emerge from your reflections. What limiting beliefs stand out the most? Consider how these beliefs have shaped your decisions, actions, and emotional responses throughout your life. This analysis will provide valuable insight into the mental barriers that have held you back.

The Next Steps:

Identifying your limiting beliefs is just the beginning. Once you have a clearer understanding of these beliefs, you can start to challenge and reframe them. Consider asking yourself questions like:

❖ Is this belief based on fact or fear?

❖ What evidence do I have that contradicts this belief?

❖ How would my life change if I let go of this belief?

By actively questioning and reframing your limiting beliefs, you begin to dismantle their power over you. This process takes time and effort, but it is essential for unlocking your potential and creating a life that aligns with your true aspirations. As you work through this journey, remember to practice self-compassion and patience. Growth is a gradual process, and every step you take toward identifying and addressing your limiting beliefs brings you closer to a more fulfilling and empowered life.

CHAPTER FOUR

CHALLENGING AND REFRAMING BELIEFS

Challenging and reframing limiting beliefs is a crucial process for personal growth and achieving one's full potential. Limiting beliefs are mental constraints that often dictate what we think we can or cannot do. These beliefs shape our behaviors, decisions, and how we approach opportunities and challenges. If left unchallenged, they can prevent us from reaching our goals, stunt personal and professional development, and lead to a life lived within unnecessary boundaries.

Actively questioning these beliefs opens the door to self-awareness and creates the opportunity to replace negative, restrictive thinking with positive, empowering beliefs. This shift in mindset is essential for building confidence, breaking free from self-sabotage, and embracing new possibilities. Reframing limiting beliefs redefines our potential, allowing us to make better choices, take more risks, and explore paths we previously thought were impossible. Reframing limiting beliefs is about taking control of your life and mindset. It enables a transformation from feeling stuck or powerless to recognizing that growth, success, and happiness are within your reach. This practice impacts your outlook and improves how you handle challenges, nurture relationships, and pursue ambitions.

Challenging Limiting Beliefs

The first step in transforming limiting beliefs is to question their validity. Many limiting beliefs are based on assumptions, misconceptions, or past experiences that no longer apply to your current situation. By actively challenging these beliefs, you open the door to new possibilities and growth.

Start by asking yourself whether the belief is grounded in fact or simply a product of negative thinking. For instance, if you believe that failure reflects your worth, take a moment to reflect on it. Is this belief truly accurate? Consider examples of others who have experienced failure and gone on to succeed. Most successful people have faced setbacks and challenges, yet they use these experiences as learning opportunities rather than allowing them to define their self-worth. When we examine our limiting beliefs, one of the most crucial questions to ask is whether these beliefs represent a universal truth or merely our personal interpretation of events. Many of us tend to treat limiting beliefs as if they are absolute, unchangeable facts about ourselves or the world. For instance, we might believe that failure is a sign of our inherent lack of ability or that making mistakes proves we are not good enough. However, when we look closer, we often find that these beliefs are not based on objective reality but rather on our own perceptions, experiences, or fears.

Failure, for example, is something everyone encounters at some point. It is part of the human experience, yet how we interpret and respond to failure differs from person to person. Some view it as a personal shortcoming, while others see it as an inevitable step on the path to success. The key difference is in how we interpret the event: those with a fixed mindset may view failure as evidence of their limitations, while those with a growth mindset understand that mistakes are simply opportunities to learn and improve. This shift in perception is powerful because it allows us to break free from the belief that failure defines our worth or capabilities.

When you question the validity of limiting beliefs, we begin to recognize them as personal interpretations rather than universal truths. This opens up space for reframing these beliefs in a way that supports growth and self-compassion. Instead of seeing mistakes as evidence of inadequacy, we can view them as valuable lessons that strengthen our resilience and guide us toward progress. In this way, limiting beliefs are not permanent roadblocks but temporary obstacles that can be challenged, reframed, and ultimately overcome. As we dismantle these self-imposed limitations, we free ourselves to embrace new possibilities and reach our full potential.

Understanding the Role of Self-Awareness In Identifying and Challenging Beliefs

Self-awareness is the cornerstone of personal growth and transformation, especially when it comes to identifying and challenging limiting beliefs. Without self-awareness, it's easy to operate on autopilot, guided by subconscious patterns of thought that shape our perceptions, actions, and outcomes. These patterns often include limiting beliefs, which can dictate how we view ourselves and the world. Developing self-awareness allows us to recognize these beliefs, understand their origins, and question their validity.

Self-awareness helps us step back and observe our thoughts without judgment. It enables us to become more conscious of how our beliefs influence our emotions and behaviors. For instance, when we encounter failure or rejection, a person lacking self-awareness might automatically assume it's a reflection of their inadequacy. However, someone with greater self-awareness would notice this negative thought pattern and investigate it. They would ask, "Is this really true?" or "Am I reacting based on past experiences rather than the present reality?" This level of introspection is crucial for breaking free from limiting beliefs, as it creates the space needed to challenge and reshape them.

It fosters emotional resilience. We can respond to situations more consciously by becoming aware of our emotional triggers and the beliefs that fuel them. Instead of reacting based on deeply ingrained fears or insecurities, we can choose to act from a place of clarity and strength. This process helps overcome limiting beliefs and empowers us to adopt more positive, empowering beliefs that align with our values and aspirations. In essence, self-awareness is the first step toward reclaiming control over our mindset and, ultimately, our lives.

Techniques for Developing Greater Self-Awareness

1. **Mindfulness Meditation:** Mindfulness meditation is one of the most effective techniques for cultivating self-awareness. By focusing on the present moment, you learn to observe your thoughts, feelings, and bodily sensations without judgment. This practice encourages you to become a neutral observer of your internal experiences, allowing you to notice the thought patterns, including limiting beliefs, that might arise. Over time, regular mindfulness practice helps you develop the skill to step back from automatic negative thinking, creating space for conscious reflection and positive change.

2. **Journaling:** Writing down your thoughts and emotions can be a powerful way to explore your inner world. You can identify recurring themes, emotional triggers, and limiting beliefs that influence your daily life through journaling. By putting these thoughts on paper, you allow yourself to analyze them from a distance, question their validity, and track your progress in overcoming them. Journaling also offers a safe space for expressing your fears, hopes, and challenges, helping you to gain clarity and insight into your belief system.

3. **Self-Reflection Exercises:** Regular self-reflection is essential for developing self awareness. Ask yourself thought-provoking questions like, "What are my beliefs about myself, my abilities, and the world?" or "How do I react to failure, criticism, or rejection?" Reflect on how these beliefs have shaped your decisions, relationships, and behavior. This process of introspection helps you uncover limiting beliefs and gives you the tools to question them. Additionally, using self-reflection at the end of each day to review your thoughts, actions, and feelings can help you identify patterns that might otherwise go unnoticed.

4. **Seeking Feedback:** Often, others can see aspects of ourselves that we may be blind to. You can gain valuable insights into how others perceive your beliefs, behaviors, and attitudes by seeking honest feedback from trusted friends, family members, or colleagues. This outside perspective can help you spot blind spots, including limiting beliefs that you might be unaware of. Receiving feedback can be a humbling experience, but it is an essential tool for developing self-awareness and growth.

5. **Body Awareness:** Our body often reflects our emotional and mental state. Paying attention to your physical responses, such as tension, tightness, or discomfort, can help you tune into underlying beliefs or emotions. For example, if you feel anxious or stressed in certain situations, take a moment to notice where you feel it in your body. Body awareness helps you stay connected to your emotions and can alert you to limiting beliefs tied to certain experiences or reactions.

Challenging Negative Self-Talk

Negative self-talk is a pervasive manifestation of limiting beliefs, often appearing as a barrage of critical or self-deprecating thoughts that undermine confidence and self-esteem. These internal dialogues can be subtle, yet their impact on our mental and emotional well-being can be profound. Challenging negative self-talk is essential in breaking free from limiting beliefs and fostering a healthier self-image. This process requires awareness, reflection, and a commitment to replacing detrimental thoughts with empowering beliefs.

The first step in addressing negative self-talk is to develop an awareness of when these critical thoughts arise. This requires mindfulness and an attentive approach to your inner dialogue. Pay attention to the words you use when speaking to yourself. Do you often use terms like "always" or "never"? Such absolutes can exaggerate negative perceptions. For example, saying "I always mess things up" overlooks past successes and reinforces a fixed mindset. Additionally, observe the tone of your self-talk. Is it harsh, sarcastic, or dismissive? Understanding the tone can help you recognize the emotional weight of your thoughts. A supportive tone can foster growth, while a critical tone can lead to self-doubt. When you catch yourself engaging in self-criticism, take a moment to pause and acknowledge these thoughts without judgment. Recognizing that you are engaging in negative self-talk is the first step toward change. This awareness allows you to step back and evaluate your thoughts rather than react impulsively.

Once you've identified negative self-talk, the next step is to question the validity of these thoughts. Assess their accuracy by asking yourself whether these negative thoughts are grounded in reality or whether they stem from fear, assumptions, or past experiences. Are you projecting past failures onto your current situation? For instance, if you believe you are not good enough to pursue a new opportunity, consider whether that belief is based on past disappointments or an objective assessment of your abilities. Investigate whether you are making assumptions that lack evidence, as many negative thoughts are based on perceived truths rather than factual evidence. For example, instead of assuming that others will judge you harshly, consider that they may be supportive or indifferent to your actions. Look for evidence that contradicts your negative self-talk.

Recall moments in your life when you succeeded or received positive feedback. This practice can help you recognize patterns that challenge your limiting beliefs and shift your perspective.

After evaluating the accuracy of your thoughts, it's time to reframe your inner narrative. Identify specific negative thoughts and create positive affirmations to counter them. For instance, if you often think, "I am not capable," reframe this to, "I am capable of learning and growing." Positive affirmations can shift your focus from what you perceive as limitations to your strengths and potential. Regularly remind yourself of your accomplishments and the qualities that make you unique. This practice can enhance your self-esteem and empower you to pursue new challenges. For example, create a list of achievements or positive feedback you have received and revisit it when you encounter negative self-talk. Visualization can also be a powerful tool in reframing your inner dialogue. Imagine yourself successfully navigating challenges and achieving your goals; this mental imagery can help solidify positive beliefs and counteract negative self-talk.

Consciously changing your self-talk can significantly improve your mental environment. Cultivating gratitude can shift your focus from negativity to appreciation. Take time each day to reflect on what you are grateful for, whether it's your skills, supportive relationships, or opportunities for growth. This practice fosters a more positive mindset. Seek positive influences through supportive friends, motivational literature, or inspiring podcasts. Engaging with uplifting content can help reinforce your positive self-talk and beliefs. Additionally, incorporate practices that promote positive self-talk into your daily routine, such as morning affirmations, mindfulness meditation, or journaling. Consistency is key to transforming your inner dialogue and creating lasting change.

Challenging negative self-talk is a transformative process that requires awareness, critical questioning, and a commitment to reframing your inner narrative. By recognizing and challenging your negative thoughts, you can replace them with positive affirmations that emphasize your strengths and potential. This shift creates a more supportive mental environment and empowers you to pursue your goals and aspirations confidently. Embrace this journey of self-discovery and allow yourself the freedom to cultivate a healthier relationship with your inner dialogue.

Challenging the Validity of Beliefs

❖ Identifying False Assumptions

Identifying false assumptions is crucial in questioning the validity of limiting beliefs. These assumptions often act as blind spots, influencing our thoughts and behaviors without us even realizing it. They can stem from past experiences, societal norms, or internalized messages that may no longer serve us. To spot untrue or outdated beliefs, consider the following strategies:

- **Examine the Origin:** Start by tracing the origins of your beliefs. Reflect on when and how you first adopted these beliefs. Were they influenced by your upbringing, traumatic experiences, or societal pressures? Understanding the context can help you recognize whether they were ever valid or if they were simply reactions to specific circumstances.

- **Challenge Generalizations:** Many limiting beliefs are based on overgeneralizations. For example, thinking, "I always fail" or "I'll never be good enough" are sweeping statements that overlook individual successes and the complexity of human experience. Challenge these generalizations by looking for evidence that contradicts them. For instance, recall instances where you succeeded or received positive feedback, and use these examples to counteract the all-encompassing negative belief.

- **Utilize Thought Records:** A practical tool for identifying false assumptions is keeping a thought record. Write down your limiting beliefs, along with the situations that triggered them. Next, analyze these thoughts by asking questions like:

   a. "What evidence supports this belief?"

   b. "What evidence contradicts it?"

   c. "Is this belief a fact or merely a perception?" This structured approach allows you to see patterns and gain perspective on the validity of your beliefs.

- **Seek Alternative Perspectives:** Discussing with others can provide new viewpoints that help challenge your limiting beliefs. Sharing your thoughts with friends, mentors, or therapists can lead to insights that help you recognize when your beliefs are based on false assumptions. For example, if you express a belief like, "I'm terrible at public speaking," a friend may remind you of a successful presentation you gave in the past, encouraging you to reevaluate your self-assessment.

- **Practice Self-Compassion:** Limiting beliefs often come with harsh self-judgment. By practicing self-compassion, you create a supportive inner dialogue that encourages exploration rather than criticism. Acknowledge that everyone has limitations and that making mistakes is a natural part of growth. This compassionate perspective allows you to question the validity of your beliefs without adding layers of shame or guilt.

Common Cognitive Distortions

Cognitive distortions are mental biases that lead us to perceive reality inaccurately, often reinforcing limiting beliefs. Here are some common cognitive distortions to watch for:

- **All-or-nothing thinking:** This distortion involves viewing situations in black-and-white terms, with no room for nuance or gray areas. For example, if you think, "If I'm not perfect, I'm a failure," you are engaging in all-or-nothing thinking. This mindset can prevent you from acknowledging incremental progress or small successes, perpetuating feelings of inadequacy.

- **Catastrophizing:** is the tendency to assume the worst possible outcome in any given situation. If you think, "If I try this and fail, it will ruin my career," you are engaging in this distortion. This kind of thinking amplifies anxiety and can lead to avoidance of challenges, preventing personal growth.

- **Overgeneralization:** This cognitive distortion occurs when you draw broad conclusions based on a single incident or limited evidence. For example, believing that you will never succeed in any future interviews because you failed one job interview is an overgeneralization that limits your potential.

- **Filtering:** Filtering involves focusing solely on the negative aspects of a situation while ignoring any positives. For instance, if you receive positive and negative feedback on a project but only dwell on the criticism, you filter out positive reinforcement that could help build your confidence.

- **Personalization:** Personalization is the belief that you are responsible for events outside your control. For example, if a friend cancels plans, you might think, "They must not want to be around me." This distortion can lead to feelings of guilt and inadequacy, reinforcing limiting beliefs about your worth.

Reframing Limiting Beliefs

Reframing is a cognitive technique that involves shifting one's perspective on a belief or situation to create a new, positive narrative. It is the process of viewing a circumstance, thought, or belief from a different angle, allowing individuals to reinterpret experiences to enhance their understanding and emotional response. By changing the way we perceive our thoughts, we can transform negative or limiting beliefs into more empowering and constructive ones.

The essence of reframing lies in recognizing that our interpretations significantly shape our emotional responses and behaviors. For instance, instead of viewing a setback as a failure, reframing allows us to see it as a learning opportunity or a stepping stone toward growth. This shift in perspective can lead to increased resilience, motivation, and a more positive outlook on life. Reframing is not about denying reality or avoiding challenges but about embracing a mindset that focuses on potential solutions and possibilities. It encourages individuals to examine their thoughts critically and challenge the validity of limiting beliefs. By adopting a reframed perspective, people can foster a sense of empowerment, enhance their problem-solving abilities, and cultivate a more optimistic approach to challenges.

Changing perspective is a powerful tool in transforming limiting beliefs into empowering ones. Our beliefs are shaped by the lens through which we view our experiences; by altering that lens, we can fundamentally change our understanding of ourselves and our capabilities. This shift can significantly impact our personal growth and development.

One effective method of changing perspective is reframing experiences. Reframing involves viewing a situation from a different angle, which can lead to new interpretations and insights. For instance, when faced with challenges, consider the positive outcomes or lessons that can emerge from the experience. If you lose a job, instead of seeing it solely as a setback, you might view it as an opportunity to explore new career paths or develop new skills. This shift in perspective helps transform a potentially negative belief about failure into a belief in resilience and adaptability. Furthermore, by contextualizing failures, we can alleviate self-blame. Recognizing that failure can stem from various external factors, such as market conditions or teamwork dynamics, allows us to foster a more compassionate view of ourselves, which can diminish the power of limiting beliefs.

Adopting a growth mindset is another powerful way to shift beliefs. A growth mindset is the belief that abilities and intelligence can be developed through effort and learning. Instead of believing that talent is fixed, focus on the importance of effort and practice. Recognizing that successful individuals often face obstacles encourages us to view challenges as growth opportunities rather than threats to our worth. Additionally, celebrating progress over perfection can counter the belief that we must achieve perfection to be worthy of success. Acknowledging the small steps we take toward our goals reinforces a more forgiving and encouraging belief system.

Engaging with diverse perspectives can also broaden our understanding and challenge existing beliefs. Surrounding ourselves with individuals who have different backgrounds, experiences, and viewpoints exposes us to new ideas and beliefs, helping us question our assumptions. By seeking diverse input, we encourage flexibility in thinking, which can dismantle rigid limiting beliefs. Practicing empathy allows us to consider the perspectives of others who have faced similar challenges or fears. Understanding how they navigated their struggles can provide insights that help reshape our beliefs. This empathetic approach fosters a sense of connection and encourages us to recognize that others have successfully overcome obstacles.

Utilizing visualization techniques can further assist in shifting beliefs by creating mental images of success and possibility. Visualizing our goals and the steps needed to achieve them helps reinforce the belief that our aspirations are attainable. For example, imagining ourselves overcoming obstacles and experiencing the success we desire can replace limiting beliefs with empowering ones. Creating a vision board is another effective tool. A vision board visually represents our goals and dreams, including images, quotes, and affirmations that resonate with our aspirations. Regularly engaging with our vision board reinforces a positive perspective on our potential and cultivates beliefs that support our journey.

Steps to Reframe Beliefs

1. Reflect on your thoughts and behaviors to recognize beliefs that hold you back. Journaling or mindfulness practices can help uncover these beliefs.

2. Question the truth of your limiting beliefs. Ask yourself if they are based on facts, assumptions, or past experiences.

3. Look for evidence that contradicts your limiting beliefs. Identify instances where you succeeded or overcame challenges, reinforcing that the belief is not accurate.

4. Create a new, positive narrative around the belief. Replace the limiting thought with an empowering statement that reflects your strengths and capabilities.

5. Picture yourself succeeding in situations related to the reframed belief. Visualization can help reinforce the new perspective and build confidence.

6. Regularly use affirmations and positive self-talk to solidify the new belief. Repeat empowering statements that align with your reframed narrative.

7. Start taking small steps toward challenging the old beliefs. Engage in activities that align with your new perspective to reinforce the belief through action.

8. Surround yourself with supportive individuals who encourage your growth and reinforce your new beliefs. Share your goals and progress with them.

9. Continuously reflect on your beliefs and experiences. If old beliefs resurface, revisit the reframing process and adjust your narrative as needed.

10. Reframing beliefs is an ongoing process that takes time and effort. Be patient with yourself and remain committed to your journey of transformation.

Technique To Reframe Limiting Beliefs

❖ Evidence Against the Belief

Gathering evidence against limiting beliefs is crucial in challenging and reframing those beliefs. Collecting tangible examples and experiences contradicting self-doubt can shift your perspective and reinforce a more empowering mindset. Here's how to effectively gather and utilize evidence to counter limiting beliefs:

Reflect on Past Achievements

One of the most compelling ways to combat limiting beliefs is to reflect on your past achievements. Consider the following strategies:

- **Create a Success Journal:** Start a journal dedicated to your successes, no matter how small. Write down achievements from various areas of your life, including personal, professional, and academic accomplishments. Documenting these victories helps create a visual reminder of your capabilities and reinforces the notion that you have succeeded before, which contradicts the belief that you are not good enough or incapable of achieving your goals.

- **Identify Specific Examples:** When recalling past successes, be specific. Instead of writing, "I did well in my job," detail the project you completed successfully, the positive feedback you received, or any recognition you earned. This specificity makes the evidence more tangible and convincing.

- **Celebrate Progress Over Perfection:** It's essential to recognize that progress is often a series of small steps rather than one monumental success. Celebrate the incremental achievements along your journey, such as learning a new skill, improving your performance in a specific task, or overcoming a challenge. These milestones can counter limiting beliefs that suggest you must achieve perfection to be worthy or successful.

Seek External Validation

Sometimes, our internal narrative can be clouded by self-doubt, making it challenging to see our worth. Seeking external validation can help counteract this:

- **Gather Feedback:** Reach out to colleagues, friends, or mentors for feedback on your abilities. Hearing positive affirmations from others can provide powerful evidence against your limiting beliefs. For instance, if you struggle with the belief that you are unqualified for a promotion, ask your manager for feedback on your contributions and areas of strength. This external perspective can help validate your skills and abilities.

- **Collect Testimonials:** If you have worked on projects or collaborated with others, ask for testimonials or recommendations. Written or verbal endorsements can serve as powerful evidence of your competence and value. These testimonials can be particularly effective in combatting feelings of inadequacy or self-doubt.

Analyze Success Stories

Looking at the successes of others who have faced similar challenges can also provide compelling evidence against limiting beliefs:

- **Research Role Models:** Identify individuals in your field or community who have overcome obstacles similar to yours. Their stories can serve as proof that success is possible despite facing self-doubt or limitations. Reflecting on their journeys can inspire you to challenge your beliefs and take action toward your goals.

- **Create a Vision Board:** A vision board featuring images and quotes from individuals who have succeeded against the odds can serve as a constant reminder that overcoming limiting beliefs is achievable. Include representations of people from diverse backgrounds who have pursued their passions, succeeded, and made significant contributions.

Reframe Failures as Learning Opportunities

Shifting the narrative around failure is essential in countering limiting beliefs. Instead of viewing failures as definitive proof of inadequacy, consider the following approaches:

- **Identify Lessons Learned:** After experiencing a setback, take the time to analyze what you learned from the situation. Ask yourself, "What can I take away from this experience?" Reframing failures as opportunities for growth allows you to extract valuable lessons that contribute to your development, contradicting the belief that failure defines your worth.

- **Create a "Failures to Success" List:** Document instances where you faced challenges or failures but later turned those experiences into successes. For example, if you initially struggled in a particular role but eventually improved through practice and dedication, record this journey. This list can serve as a tangible reminder that setbacks do not equate to being incapable, and growth is always possible.

Use Affirmations and Positive Self-Talk

Finally, incorporate affirmations and positive self-talk to solidify the evidence against limiting beliefs:

- **Craft Affirmative Statements:** Create positive affirmations that counteract your limiting beliefs. For example, if your belief is, "I am not good enough to pursue my dreams," reframe it to, "I am capable and worthy of achieving my goals." Regularly recite these affirmations to reinforce a positive mindset.

- **Practice Positive Self-Talk:** Replace negative self-talk with constructive and supportive language. Instead of thinking, "I'll never succeed," remind yourself, "I have the skills and resources to learn and grow." This shift in self-dialogue can help solidify the evidence you've gathered against limiting beliefs.

Gathering evidence to contradict limiting beliefs creates a robust foundation for growth and empowerment. This process encourages a shift from self-doubt to self-confidence, fostering a mindset that embraces challenges and seeks opportunities for learning and success. As you work to gather evidence and counteract limiting beliefs, remember that personal growth is a journey, and every step taken towards challenging these beliefs is a step toward unlocking your full potential.

CHAPTER FIVE

THE POWER OF MINDSET SHIFTS

Understanding Mindset

Mindset refers to the underlying beliefs and attitudes that shape our perceptions, behaviors, and experiences. It serves as the lens through which we interpret the world and make sense of our experiences. What's crucial to understand is that mindsets are not fixed; they are dynamic and adaptable constructs that can be cultivated and changed over time.

Mindset shifts refer to fundamental changes in thinking and perceiving our abilities, experiences, and potential. They represent a transformation in our underlying beliefs and attitudes, often leading to new ways of interpreting challenges and opportunities. At the heart of mindset shifts is the distinction between fixed and growth mindsets. A fixed mindset assumes that our abilities and intelligence are static and unchangeable, leading to a fear of failure and a reluctance to embrace challenges. In contrast, a growth mindset embraces the belief that our abilities can be developed through dedication, hard work, and learning from experiences. This shift in perspective is crucial for personal growth and can significantly impact our overall well-being, relationships, and success in various areas of life.

Shifting our mindset involves recognizing and challenging limiting beliefs that hold us back. It requires a willingness to confront discomfort and uncertainty and the courage to step outside our comfort zones. As we adopt a growth mindset, we open ourselves up to new possibilities and a greater capacity for resilience. This chapter will explore the science behind mindset shifts, practical strategies for cultivating a growth mindset, and the powerful impact these shifts can have on our lives.

There are two primary types of mindsets: fixed mindsets and growth mindsets. These mindsets differ in their beliefs about capabilities, possibilities, and change, influencing how we approach challenges and opportunities.

Fixed Mindset

A fixed mindset is characterized by the belief that skills and intelligence are static and unchanging. People with a fixed mindset often believe their talents and abilities are innate and cannot be developed further. As a result, they tend to avoid challenges for fear of failure or criticism. This mindset is associated with limiting beliefs, a lack of self-confidence, and a fear of failure. It fosters a mental framework that values performance over learning, leading to a reluctance to take risks or pursue growth opportunities. A fixed mindset can stifle creativity, innovation, and progress, limiting the capacity to learn and grow. This mindset leads to several key behaviors and thought patterns:

1. **Fear of Failure:** Individuals with a fixed mindset are often paralyzed by the fear of making mistakes. They may see failure as a reflection of their self-worth, leading them to shy away from situations where they might not excel.

2. **Avoidance of Challenges:** To protect their sense of self, those with a fixed mindset often avoid challenges altogether. They may choose easier tasks that guarantee success, which limits their growth and potential.

3. **Defensiveness in Criticism:** When faced with criticism or feedback, individuals with a fixed mindset may become defensive, perceiving feedback as a personal attack rather than a chance to improve. This defensiveness inhibits learning and stunts personal development.

4. **Limited View of Success:** Success is often defined in narrow terms, such as achieving certain grades or accolades. This can create a cycle of seeking validation through external achievements rather than valuing the learning process itself.

Growth Mindset

A growth mindset, on the other hand, is defined by the belief that skills and intelligence can be developed through effort, learning, and perseverance. Individuals with a growth mindset embrace challenges, seeing them as opportunities for growth and self-improvement. A growth mindset fosters a mental framework that prioritizes learning over performance, making it easier to embrace change and uncertainty positively. Adopting a growth mindset can significantly influence personal and professional development, leading to a more fulfilling and successful life.

Characteristics of a Growth Mindset

1. **Embracing Challenges:** Individuals with a growth mindset view challenges as opportunities to learn and grow rather than obstacles to avoid. They understand that stepping outside their comfort zones is essential for personal development. For example, a student might take on a difficult subject or a new project at work, knowing that the effort required will lead to valuable learning experiences.

2. **Persistence in the Face of Setbacks:** A hallmark of a growth mindset is resilience. When faced with setbacks or failures, individuals with a growth mindset are more likely to persist. They see failure as a natural part of the learning process, using it to reflect on what went wrong and how they can improve. This resilience allows them to bounce back from disappointments and continue striving for their goals.

3. **Learning from Feedback:** People with a growth mindset actively seek out and embrace constructive feedback. They view criticism as an opportunity for growth rather than a personal attack. By welcoming feedback, they can identify areas for improvement and make necessary adjustments to enhance their skills and performance.

4. **Celebrating Others' Successes:** Instead of feeling threatened or jealous of others' achievements, individuals with a growth mindset find inspiration in the success of others. They understand that learning from peers can provide valuable insights and motivation. This collaborative spirit fosters a sense of community and support, enabling individuals to grow together.

5. **Focus on Effort Over Talent:** Those with a growth mindset emphasize the importance of effort, practice, and persistence in achieving success. They believe hard work is critical to developing skills and abilities. This focus shifts the

narrative away from innate talent, reinforcing the idea that anyone can improve through dedication and practice.

How Mindset Influences Behavior

Mindsets are crucial in shaping our behavior, determining how we approach challenges, make decisions, and interact with others. They act as lenses through which we interpret experiences and formulate responses, ultimately guiding our actions and reactions in various situations. This section explores how mindset influences our perception of success and failure, our responses to setbacks, and our ability to adapt to change.

1. Perception of Success and Failure

Mindset significantly impacts how we perceive success and failure. Individuals with a fixed mindset often view failure as a definitive judgment of their abilities or worth, leading to feelings of helplessness and self-doubt. They may believe that their talents and intelligence are static traits, causing them to avoid challenges that might expose their perceived inadequacies. This perspective can create a cycle of fear and avoidance, where the prospect of failure becomes paralyzing, hindering personal and professional growth.

In contrast, those with a growth mindset embrace failure as a vital component of the learning process. They see setbacks as opportunities to gather insights and develop new skills. This positive outlook encourages them to approach challenges with curiosity and perseverance. For example, instead of fearing failure, individuals with a growth mindset may experiment, take risks, and reflect on their experiences, ultimately fostering resilience and adaptability. By reframing their perception of success and failure, they cultivate a sense of agency that empowers them to pursue their goals with enthusiasm and determination.

2. Response to Setbacks

Mindset also profoundly affects how we respond to setbacks. People with a fixed mindset may struggle to recover from adversity, often feeling defeated, overwhelmed, or demoralized. They might quickly give up when faced with challenges, viewing setbacks as confirmations of their limitations rather than stepping stones toward success. This response can lead to a lack of motivation and a reluctance to try new approaches, perpetuating a cycle of stagnation.

Conversely, those with a growth mindset tend to view setbacks as opportunities for improvement. They are more likely to apply adaptive coping strategies, such as problem solving, seeking support, and maintaining a positive outlook. By analyzing what went wrong and considering alternative strategies, they can learn from their experiences and continue to persevere in the face of difficulties. This resilience enables them to bounce back from setbacks more quickly and emerge stronger, reinforcing their belief in their capacity for growth and change.

3. Ability to Adapt to Change

Their mindset significantly influences a person's ability to adapt to change and uncertainty. Those with a fixed mindset may resist change, fearing the unknown and the potential for failure. They might cling to familiar routines and established ways of thinking, which can stifle innovation and personal growth. This resistance can create a sense of discomfort and anxiety in the face of new challenges, ultimately limiting their opportunities for advancement.

On the other hand, individuals with a growth mindset welcome change as an opportunity for learning and personal development. They are more open to new experiences, ideas, and perspectives, viewing change as a natural part of life's journey. This adaptability allows them to navigate transitions with confidence and flexibility, positioning them to thrive in dynamic environments. By embracing change, they enhance their problem-solving abilities and resilience, fostering a sense of empowerment that propels them toward success.

4. The Power of Changing Your Mindset

The power of changing your mindset lies in its capacity to transform your perceptions and behaviors. By shifting from a fixed mindset to a growth mindset, you free yourself from limiting beliefs and open the door to a life rooted in growth, resilience, and empowerment. This shift encourages you to take on challenges with enthusiasm, view failures as valuable lessons, and embrace change as an opportunity for personal development.

Developing a growth mindset enables you to adopt a more adaptive and resilient approach to challenges, fostering both personal and collective growth. This mindset encourages collaboration, creativity, and innovation, as individuals are more likely to share ideas and support each other in their journeys. As you cultivate a growth mindset, you not only enhance your own potential but also contribute to a more supportive and dynamic environment, inspiring others to embrace their paths of growth and transformation.

Adopting a Growth Mindset

Adopting a growth mindset requires self-awareness, commitment, and a willingness to challenge deeply rooted beliefs. By understanding how our mindset shapes our behavior, we can harness the power of our brains to create lasting change and personal empowerment.

To cultivate a growth mindset, consider the following strategies:

- Embrace challenges: Recognize challenges as opportunities for learning and development rather than threats to your capabilities.

- Learn from mistakes: View mistakes as valuable lessons that contribute to your growth, rather than as signs of failure.

- Focus on effort over talent: Shift your focus from innate ability to the effort and persistence you put into achieving your goals.

- Cultivate curiosity: Foster a sense of curiosity and openness to new experiences, ideas, and opportunities for growth.

- Practice self-compassion: Treat yourself with kindness and understanding in moments of failure or struggle, reinforcing your belief in your ability to grow.

By adopting these strategies, you can begin to shift your mindset from fixed to growth, unlocking greater potential for personal achievement and fulfillment. Embracing a growth mindset allows you to approach life's challenges with confidence, resilience, and an unwavering belief in your ability to succeed.

Challenge Strong Beliefs

One of the first steps toward personal growth is identifying and challenging strong beliefs about your abilities and potential. These deeply held convictions often shape the way we see ourselves and the world around us. For instance, if someone believes they are not good at public speaking, this belief may lead them to avoid opportunities for presentations or discussions, ultimately limiting their professional growth and interpersonal connections. Questioning the validity of these beliefs is essential for breaking free from their constraints. Are these beliefs based on solid evidence, or are they limiting perceptions shaped by past experiences, failures, or negative feedback?

Exploring alternative perspectives that align with a growth mindset can be beneficial to challenge strong beliefs effectively. This involves reframing negative thoughts into more positive, constructive ones. For example, instead of saying, "I will never be able to do this," one might reframe it as, "I may not know how to do this yet, but I can learn." Doing so opens ourselves to new possibilities and develops a more empowering view of our potential. This shift in perspective encourages personal growth and enhances our resilience in facing challenges.

❖ **Embrace Challenges**

Challenges should not be viewed as obstacles to avoid but rather as opportunities to grow and develop. Approaching challenges with curiosity and determination allows us to see them as a necessary part of our journey toward personal improvement. For instance, when faced with a difficult project at work, instead of feeling overwhelmed, we can approach it enthusiastically, viewing it as a chance to learn new skills and broaden our expertise.

Embracing the learning process—rather than focusing solely on performance—fosters resilience and perseverance. This means shifting our mindset from a narrow focus on success or failure to a broader understanding of the developmental benefits gained from the experience. With each challenge we face, we develop skills, gain insights, and become better equipped to handle future difficulties. This approach ultimately shifts our focus from immediate outcomes to long-term personal development, making us more adaptable and capable individuals.

❖ **Learn from Mistakes**

Mistakes are inevitable, but how we respond to them can make all the difference in our growth journey. A growth mindset encourages us to view mistakes as opportunities for learning rather than signs of failure. For instance, if someone attempts to start a new business and fails, rather than succumbing to discouragement, they can analyze what went wrong and apply those lessons to future endeavors.

Reflecting on the lessons learned from setbacks helps us make better decisions in the future. Each misstep can become a stepping stone to success when we use it to guide our actions and refine our approach. This perspective transforms the narrative from fear of failure to an ongoing process of growth. By cultivating a mindset that embraces mistakes as valuable learning experiences, we foster resilience, adaptability, and an eagerness to pursue our goals with renewed determination.

❖ **Encourage Curiosity**

Curiosity serves as the gateway to creativity and innovation. Encouraging curiosity allows us to explore new ideas, perspectives, and experiences, thereby broadening our understanding of the world. When we cultivate a curious mindset, we become more willing to step outside of our comfort zones and welcome different viewpoints. This openness nurtures a mindset that is conducive to continuous learning and improvement, which is vital for personal growth.

For example, engaging in new hobbies, pursuing diverse interests, or seeking experiences that challenge our beliefs can stimulate our curiosity. This willingness to learn from others and explore various perspectives enriches our lives and promotes a sense of adaptability and evolution. This mindset becomes essential for thriving in a constantly changing environment, as it helps us navigate uncertainty and embrace new possibilities. By fostering curiosity, we create an enriching foundation for lifelong learning and personal development, empowering us to adapt and flourish in our ever-evolving world.

Pursuing Your Goals and Aspirations

A growth mindset empowers you to pursue your goals and aspirations with unwavering determination. It helps you overcome limiting beliefs and self-doubt by fostering a belief in your ability to grow and improve. To approach your goals with a growth-oriented mindset, consider these strategies:

- Set growth-minded goals: Focus on goals that are aligned with your values and emphasize development over mere performance. This way, your goals serve as a roadmap for both personal and professional growth.

- Embrace the learning process: Approach challenges with a sense of curiosity, viewing setbacks as valuable learning experiences. Celebrate effort and persistence rather than just achievement.

- Celebrate progress: Acknowledge each small victory along the way. Recognizing your progress fuels motivation and reinforces your commitment to your aspirations.

Overcoming Challenges and Setbacks

With a growth mindset, challenges and setbacks become opportunities for growth rather than reasons for despair. By adopting a growth-oriented approach, you can view obstacles as valuable lessons and use them to inform your future decisions. To overcome challenges with resilience, keep these strategies in mind:

- Embrace change and uncertainty: See change not as a threat, but as an opportunity to learn. Uncertainty provides the chance to develop new skills and broaden your perspective.

- Use adaptive coping strategies: Focus on problem-solving and emotional regulation when managing stress and adversity. Developing healthy coping mechanisms helps maintain emotional balance in difficult situations.

- Promote resilience: Building resilience is key to navigating life's ups and downs. A growth mindset fosters a positive outlook, allowing you to face setbacks with confidence and determination.

Future Directions

The power of actionable strategies is a transformative force that can shape both our lives and the world around us. By understanding how our beliefs and mindsets influence our behavior, we can harness this power to overcome limiting beliefs, build resilience, and achieve our goals. This journey requires courage, commitment, and a willingness to confront the beliefs that no longer serve us.

As we embark on this path, it is essential to develop self-awareness, compassion, and resilience. By accepting our true selves and reframing our beliefs, we can create a life that is aligned with our core values and aspirations. The journey of self-empowerment is ongoing—a continuous process of learning, growth, and transformation that offers endless opportunities for personal and collective development.

In the chapters ahead, we will explore how to build resilience and overcome setbacks, examine the impact of our beliefs and mindsets on our actions, and equip ourselves with practical tools and techniques for creating a life that is in harmony with our values. Through self-awareness, introspection, and a commitment to growth, you can unlock your potential and take the first steps toward self-determination.

CHAPTER SIX

ACTIONABLE STRATEGIES FOR CHANGE

Change is essential to personal growth and empowerment, offering countless opportunities for transformation, learning, and development. Although embracing change can be challenging, it serves as one of the most powerful catalysts for growth, resilience, and fulfillment. Change allows us to evolve beyond limiting beliefs and outdated mindsets, allowing for new perspectives and possibilities. By navigating the discomfort that often accompanies change, we unlock our potential, develop new skills, and shape our lives in ways that align with our values and aspirations.

We gain practical tools to navigate the inevitable challenges and obstacles accompanying change by implementing actionable strategies to reframe limiting beliefs. These strategies include self-reflection, mindfulness practices, and the cultivation of a growth mindset—all essential elements for overcoming resistance to change and expanding our horizons. For instance, self-reflection helps us recognize how our beliefs and thoughts shape our behavior, while mindfulness enables us to remain present and observe our internal dialogue without judgment. This awareness is crucial for identifying limiting beliefs and choosing new perspectives to serve our growth.

The Nature of Change

Change is a dynamic and continuous process that allows us to grow, learn, and evolve. It is an inherent part of life, shaping every experience and opportunity we encounter. While it can often be uncomfortable or unsettling, change is essential for both personal and collective development, which propels us forward. With change, growth continues, and we become stuck in patterns that no longer serve us, limiting our potential to explore new possibilities or achieve our goals.

Embracing change opens the door to new opportunities, challenges, and avenues for learning. Change requires us to step outside our comfort zones and face the unknown, whether it's a career shift, personal transformation, or adapting to life's uncertainties. It pushes us to develop new skills, gain fresh perspectives, and tap into previously untapped potential. Change challenges our beliefs, tests our resilience, and ultimately expands our understanding of ourselves and the world around us.

Though challenges and setbacks often accompany change, precisely these obstacles serve as powerful drivers for resilience and empowerment. Whether personal or professional, difficult transitions force us to confront our fears, insecurities, and limiting beliefs. However, by facing these challenges, we learn to adapt, problem-solve, and grow stronger as a result. Each setback presents an opportunity to develop emotional resilience—the capacity to recover and thrive in the face of adversity. This resilience is crucial for navigating future challenges and building the confidence and strength needed to pursue bigger dreams and aspirations.

One of the key aspects of embracing change is accepting uncertainty. Human beings naturally seek stability and predictability, but life is inherently uncertain. When we learn to embrace this uncertainty rather than resist it, we unlock a new level of growth and personal freedom. By acknowledging that we cannot control every outcome, we can let go of the fear of the unknown and instead focus on what we can control—our mindset, our actions, and our responses to change. This shift in perspective allows us to approach challenges with curiosity, flexibility, and openness to learning. In embracing change, we also align our lives more closely with our values and aspirations. Our priorities, goals, and desires may shift as we evolve and grow. By accepting and welcoming change, we permit ourselves to adjust course when necessary, pursuing paths that are more fulfilling and aligned with our true selves. This alignment process strengthens us individually and contributes to the development of those around us. When we model adaptability, resilience, and a growth-oriented mindset, we inspire others to do the same, creating positive change within our communities and relationships.

Change is a powerful force for transformation. It challenges us to evolve beyond our current limitations, build resilience, and create a life that reflects our values and aspirations. While it may bring uncertainty and discomfort, change offers the potential for limitless growth and opportunity.

Assessing the Need for Change

Recognizing When Change is Necessary

Change can be both daunting and empowering. Often, people find themselves stuck in routines or situations that no longer serve their best interests, yet they continue to remain in these spaces due to fear, comfort, or simply not realizing that change is needed. However, assessing when a shift is necessary is crucial for personal and professional growth. Recognizing the signs that change is required involves self-awareness, external observation, and honest reflection.

Signs That Change is Necessary

1. **Stagnation**

   A clear indication that change is needed is the feeling of stagnation. This can manifest as a need for growth in life's personal, professional, or emotional aspects. When the routine becomes monotonous and no progress seems to be made, it's often a sign that something needs to shift. For example, staying in a job for years without learning new skills or being in a relationship that doesn't foster growth may indicate it's time to reevaluate and make changes.

2. **Persistent Discontent**

   When feelings of dissatisfaction or frustration are constantly present, it can be a red flag. If everyday experiences feel draining or unfulfilling despite efforts to change your attitude or approach, the underlying situation may need to change. For instance, if someone is frequently unhappy in their work environment or with their current lifestyle, it could signal that it's time to consider new opportunities or lifestyle adjustments.

3. **Lack of Alignment with Core Values**

When your actions, surroundings, or relationships no longer align with your core values and beliefs, it's an indication that change is necessary. Staying in situations that conflict with your true self leads to internal discord. For example, if you value creativity but work in a job that stifles expression, or if personal relationships conflict with your integrity, a change might be needed to restore balance and fulfillment.

4. **Chronic Stress and Fatigue**

Prolonged stress, exhaustion, or burnout can signal that certain aspects of life are unsustainable. While occasional stress is normal, chronic stress without relief points to a deeper issue. Persistent stress can drain energy and motivation, whether it's a demanding job, a toxic relationship, or an unhealthy lifestyle. Recognizing these physical and emotional cues is critical in identifying the need for change to protect your well-being.

5. **Unmet Goals and Aspirations**

When your personal or professional goals still need to be met despite the effort, it may indicate that the current environment or approach could be more conducive to achieving success. If you're constantly feeling blocked from realizing your ambitions, assessing whether change is necessary to open new doors and paths forward might be time.

6. **Negative Impact on Health or Well-Being**

Physical symptoms, such as frequent headaches, insomnia, or changes in appetite, can sometimes be linked to emotional or mental strain. If a situation consistently affects your physical health, it's a sign that something must change. When the body is often overwhelmed, it reflects the need for emotional or situational adjustments.

7. **Feedback from Others**

Sometimes, those around us can see the need for change before we do. If trusted friends, colleagues, or family members consistently point out areas in our lives that are holding us back or causing us distress, it is worth considering their input. Listening to constructive feedback can help us gain insight into aspects of our lives that need change.

How Beliefs and Mindsets Affect Change

Beliefs and mindsets shape how we perceive and respond to change. They influence our ability to tackle challenges, overcome obstacles, and interact with the world. By understanding the role of beliefs and mindsets in shaping our behavior, we can harness the power of our brains to create lasting change and empower ourselves to achieve our goals.

❖ Beliefs and Change

Beliefs are the mental frameworks we construct to make sense of the world, our place in it, and how things should function. These deeply ingrained perceptions often form in early life, shaped by our upbringing, culture, experiences, and even societal expectations. Once established, beliefs tend to guide our thoughts, feelings, and behaviors—often without conscious awareness. In this way, beliefs act as invisible lenses through which we view opportunities, challenges, relationships, and even our self-worth.

However, beliefs can either **support** or **hinder** the process of change. When our beliefs are empowering, they can propel us toward success and growth. But when our beliefs are limiting, they create significant barriers to achieving change and personal transformation.

How Beliefs Influence Behavior and Change

1. **Beliefs Shape Identity**

   Our belief system is at the core of who we are, which fundamentally influences our identity. What we believe about ourselves—whether we see ourselves as capable, worthy, intelligent, or talented—directly informs how we approach challenges and the change process. For example, if someone believes they are resilient and adaptable, they are more likely to embrace change positively. Conversely, if someone believes they are not good enough or that change will inevitably lead to failure, they will likely resist or avoid change altogether.

2. **Beliefs Inform Our Perception of What's Possible**

    Our beliefs play a critical role in determining what we believe is achievable. If you believe that you're limited by external circumstances, lack of skills, or other factors, you may avoid taking risks or pursuing opportunities for growth. On the other hand, if you believe in your ability to learn, adapt, and overcome, you're more likely to take bold steps toward personal or professional development.

    For example, a person who believes they "aren't good at public speaking" may avoid opportunities to develop this skill, missing out on chances to improve. However, if they challenge this belief and replace it with, "I can learn to become a confident speaker with practice," they can take actionable steps toward growth.

3. **Beliefs Dictate Emotional Reactions to Change**

    The emotions we experience in response to change often reflect our underlying beliefs. Someone who believes that change is inherently risky and dangerous will feel anxiety or fear in the face of new circumstances. Alternatively, someone who views change as an opportunity for growth and learning will likely approach it with excitement or curiosity. This emotional response shapes how we engage with the process of change, either motivating us to move forward or causing us to retreat into familiar, comfortable patterns.

Limiting beliefs are negative assumptions we hold about ourselves or the world that prevent us from pursuing our potential. These beliefs are often rooted in fear, self-doubt, or past negative experiences. Common limiting beliefs include:

- "I'm not good enough."

- "I'll fail if I try something new."

- "Change is too difficult or risky."

- "Other people can succeed, but I can't."

These beliefs create mental roadblocks that stop us from taking the necessary actions to initiate or sustain change. They manifest as self-sabotaging behaviors such as procrastination, indecision, or avoidance. For example, someone who believes they need to be more others may avoid taking on leadership roles, even when opportunities arise. This perpetuates a cycle of self fulfilling prophecy, where limiting beliefs continue to restrict growth.

Self-doubt and negative self-talk are among the most destructive effects of limiting beliefs. Constant internal dialogue like "I'm not smart enough" or "I can't handle this" chips away at confidence, undermines motivation and diminishes the desire to embrace change. The more we internalize these beliefs, the more difficult it becomes to see ourselves as capable of transformation.

Self-awareness and introspection are essential to overcoming limiting beliefs. This involves examining and questioning our beliefs and then transforming them into empowering beliefs that support our growth and progress. Doing so can remove the mental barriers that prevent us from embracing change and achieving success.

❖ **Mindset and Change: The Power of Perspective**

Mindset refers to the underlying attitudes, beliefs, and assumptions that influence how we view and respond to the world around us. It plays a crucial role in determining how we approach challenges, opportunities, and change. Our mindset shapes how we perceive obstacles, interact with others, and engage in new experiences. In the context of change, mindset can either be a powerful ally, helping us embrace transformation or a significant barrier that keeps us stuck in old patterns.

The power of mindset lies in its capacity to shift our perspectives and behaviors. By developing a mindset that supports growth and adaptability, we can break free from limiting beliefs and embrace change as a personal and professional development tool. A key aspect of this is recognizing the difference between a fixed mindset and a growth mindset and understanding how cultivating the latter can enhance our ability to thrive in the face of change.

The Role of Mindset in Embracing Change

Mindset is a powerful determinant of how we handle change. It influences our ability to move beyond our comfort zones, take risks, and develop new skills. By adopting a growth mindset, individuals can transform their relationship with change, seeing it not as a threat but as an opportunity for growth, learning, and self-discovery.

1. **Mindset and Adaptability**

   One of the most important aspects of successfully navigating change is adaptability—the ability to adjust to new circumstances and embrace the unknown. A growth mindset fosters adaptability by encouraging openness to new ideas, flexibility in thinking, and a willingness to learn from experiences, even when they are difficult.

   People with a growth mindset are more likely to embrace uncertainty and ambiguity, which are often inherent in periods of change. Instead of clinging to the familiar or resisting new situations, they see change as an opportunity to develop new skills and gain fresh perspectives. This adaptability allows them to thrive in environments that require continuous learning and adjustment.

2. **Mindset and Resilience**

   Resilience is another critical factor in how we respond to change. A growth mindset encourages resilience by helping individuals view setbacks as temporary and surmountable. Those with a growth mindset don't give up easily when faced with challenges. Instead, they learn from their mistakes and use them as fuel to keep moving forward.

This resilience is particularly important during times of change when setbacks or obstacles are inevitable. Rather than being discouraged by failure, individuals with a growth mindset see it as a natural part of the learning process. They are more likely to persist in the face of adversity, ultimately emerging stronger and more capable.

3. **Mindset and the Willingness to Take Risks**

Change often involves stepping into the unknown and taking risks. A growth mindset encourages individuals to take calculated risks and pursue new opportunities, even when success is not guaranteed. This willingness to step outside one's comfort zone is essential for personal and professional growth.

In contrast, a fixed mindset can lead to risk aversion, as individuals fear failure or believe they cannot succeed in new situations. By fostering a growth mindset, individuals become more comfortable with uncertainty and are willing to take the necessary risks to embrace change and move forward.

Actionable Strategies for Change

Actionable strategies for change provide practical tools and techniques for mastering challenges, overcoming obstacles, and creating a life that aligns with our values and aspirations. By adopting these strategies, we empower ourselves to achieve lasting personal growth and success.

❖ Goal Setting and Planning

Goal setting and planning are fundamental components of change. They provide a clear, structured framework for pursuing goals and aspirations, ensuring that our efforts are purposeful and aligned with our values. By setting SMART goals—specific, measurable, achievable, relevant, and time-bound—we create a roadmap for success that guides our actions and decisions.

Consider the following strategies for effective goal setting and planning:

- Define Your Goals: Identify your goals and aspirations, focusing on what truly matters to you. Reflect on your values, passions, and priorities, and use these to set meaningful and fulfilling goals.

- Create a Plan: Develop a plan for achieving your goals by breaking them down into manageable steps and milestones. Identify the resources, skills, and support you'll need and incorporate them into your plan.

- Track Your Progress: Regularly track your progress and celebrate your accomplishments. Recognize the value of your efforts and perseverance, using your successes as motivation to continue pursuing your goals.

❖ **Time Management and Productivity**

Effective time management and productivity strategies are essential for navigating change. They enable us to prioritize tasks, manage resources, and maintain focus on our goals. Developing these strategies helps us build balanced and fulfilling lives while fostering personal and collective growth.

Consider the following strategies for improving time management and productivity:

- Prioritize Tasks: Identify the most important tasks that align with your goals and values. Focus your energy on these tasks to ensure that your time is spent on what matters most.

- Create a Schedule: Develop a daily or weekly schedule that includes dedicated time for your goals. Use time-blocking or similar techniques to ensure that your priorities receive consistent attention.

- Minimize Distractions: Identify potential distractions that may derail your productivity and take steps to minimize them. This may involve setting boundaries, limiting time spent on non-essential activities, or creating an environment conducive to focus.

❖ Cultivating Resilience

Resilience is the ability to bounce back from challenges and setbacks, and it plays a critical role in personal growth. By cultivating resilience, we develop the mental and emotional strength needed to navigate change and continue moving forward in the face of adversity.

Here are strategies to cultivate resilience:

- Develop Emotional Awareness: Pay attention to your emotions, recognizing them without judgment. Emotional awareness helps you process challenges in a healthy way.

- Practice Mindfulness: Incorporate mindfulness practices, such as meditation, into your daily routine to reduce stress and improve emotional regulation.

- Embrace Change: View change as an opportunity rather than a threat. You build mental flexibility and resilience by adopting a positive attitude toward change.

Time Management and Productivity Strategies

Time management and productivity are critical to achieving personal and professional success. When you manage your time effectively, you can focus on what truly matters, reduce stress, and create a sense of control over your daily activities. Productivity strategies allow you to maximize the impact of your efforts, ensuring that your time is spent on meaningful tasks that move you closer to your goals. Implementing specific time management techniques can significantly enhance your ability to accomplish more in less time.

One of the foundational strategies is prioritizing your tasks. By focusing on what is most important, you can ensure that your time is aligned with your long-term goals and values. A useful tool in this process is a priority matrix or to-do list, which helps categorize tasks by importance and urgency. This approach allows you to allocate your time and energy efficiently, tackling high-priority tasks first and avoiding the trap of being consumed by less significant activities. Prioritization also prevents you from feeling overwhelmed by minor tasks, making your day more manageable and productive.

Setting clear boundaries is another essential aspect of time management. Protecting your time and energy by establishing limits on your availability is crucial for preventing burnout and maintaining focus on the most meaningful tasks. One effective technique is time blocking, where you schedule specific periods in your day for different types of work, rest, and personal activities. This structure ensures that important tasks receive dedicated attention and are kept from being crowded out by less critical ones. By setting boundaries on when and how you work, you create a balanced schedule that fosters both productivity and well-being.

Minimizing distractions is equally important in maintaining focus and productivity. In a world filled with constant interruptions—whether from social media, phone calls, or emails—staying focused requires conscious effort. Techniques like the Pomodoro Technique, which involves working in focused intervals (typically 25 minutes of work followed by a 5-minute break), can help maintain concentration and reduce mental fatigue. Combining this with time-blocking strategies enables you to stay on task and avoid distractions throughout the day. You create a productive atmosphere that supports efficient work by intentionally managing your environment and limiting interruptions.

By integrating these time management and productivity strategies into your daily routine, you can increase your focus, improve efficiency, and ultimately achieve more while reducing stress and maintaining balance in your life.

Regulation and Stress Management

Emotion regulation and stress management are crucial for maintaining personal well-being and fostering growth. When we learn to manage our emotions effectively and reduce stress, we create a stable foundation to navigate life's challenges with resilience and grace. Developing these skills enhances our mental health and improves our relationships, decision-making, and overall quality of life.

One of the most effective strategies for emotion regulation and stress management is mindfulness and meditation. Mindfulness involves staying present in the moment, which allows us to observe our thoughts and feelings without judgment. By incorporating practices such as deep breathing, body scanning, and guided meditation, we can reduce the physiological symptoms of stress and regain emotional control. These techniques help calm the mind and body, creating space for thoughtful responses rather than impulsive reactions. Regular mindfulness practice has been shown to improve emotional awareness, helping individuals respond to challenges with greater clarity and composure.

Self-compassion and self-care are also essential components of managing stress and emotions. During difficult times, it's easy to be critical of ourselves or neglect our own needs. However, treating ourselves with kindness, understanding, and patience is key to maintaining emotional stability. Self-compassion involves recognizing our humanity and imperfections, allowing us to face challenges without undue self-blame. At the same time, self-care practices—such as ensuring adequate rest, relaxation, and engaging in activities that promote mental and physical health—are vital for maintaining balance.

Prioritizing these practices helps prevent burnout and promotes emotional resilience, enabling us to handle stress more effectively.

Additionally, cultivating gratitude and practicing positive psychology significantly affect emotion regulation. Focusing on what we are thankful for and acknowledging our strengths and achievements can shift our mindset from negativity to appreciation and positivity. Regularly reflecting on the good in our lives helps foster a sense of emotional well-being and boosts our capacity to cope with stress. This positive focus doesn't ignore the challenges we face but allows us to approach them with a more balanced and empowered outlook. Expressing gratitude can significantly improve emotional resilience, enabling us to stay grounded and optimistic even in difficult situations.

By integrating these emotion regulation and stress management strategies—mindfulness, self-compassion, self-care, and gratitude—we build the emotional tools necessary to manage stress, maintain balance, and support our personal growth. These approaches help create a sense of calm and emotional clarity, allowing us to thrive in both everyday situations and in the face of adversity.

The Impact of Actionable Strategies on Personal Growth

Adopting actionable strategies for change has a profound impact on personal growth. These strategies empower us to pursue our goals, overcome challenges, and experience a deeper sense of fulfillment. By integrating these approaches into our lives, we can align our actions with our values, foster resilience, and enhance self-determination.

Pursuing your goals and aspirations becomes more manageable with actionable strategies in place. Setting growth-oriented goals, rather than performance-based ones, ensures that your focus is on personal development rather than merely achieving outcomes. When you embrace the learning process and treat setbacks as opportunities for growth, you build the perseverance needed to succeed in the long term. Celebrate progress along the way, acknowledging the value of effort and determination as you work toward your aspirations.

Overcoming challenges and setbacks is another benefit of adopting actionable strategies. By viewing obstacles as opportunities for growth, you can approach difficulties with resilience and adaptability. Embracing change and uncertainty, as well as employing adaptive coping strategies, allows you to manage stress and adversity effectively. Developing a positive mindset, in combination with adaptive coping mechanisms, fosters resilience and helps you rise above setbacks with confidence.

Future Directions

The power of actionable strategies lies in their ability to create lasting change in both our personal lives and the world around us. By understanding how deeply held beliefs and mindsets influence our behavior, we can consciously reshape our perspectives to overcome limiting beliefs, build resilience, and pursue our goals with clarity and determination. This process requires courage, introspection, and a willingness to challenge the beliefs and patterns that no longer serve us.

As we move forward on this transformative journey, self-awareness, compassion, and resilience are essential companions. Developing self-awareness allows us to recognize the beliefs that shape our actions, while self-compassion helps us navigate the challenges we face without judgment. Resilience enables us to persevere in the face of setbacks, learning from our experiences and emerging stronger. Together, these qualities empower us to align our lives with our core values and aspirations, creating a path forward that is authentic and fulfilling.

The journey of self-empowerment is not a one-time event but an ongoing process of growth, learning, and transformation. It offers countless opportunities to refine our approach, deepen our understanding, and elevate our potential. Each step we take brings us closer to a life that reflects who we truly are and what we value most.

In the chapters ahead, we will explore practical strategies for building resilience, overcoming obstacles, and understanding the profound impact of our beliefs and mindsets on our actions. We will equip ourselves with tools and techniques to create a life that resonates with our values, fostering a sense of purpose and fulfillment. Through introspection, self-awareness, and a commitment to continuous growth, you can unlock your potential and take decisive steps toward self-determination and empowerment.

CHAPTER SEVEN

BUILDING RESILIENCE AND OVERCOMING SETBACKS

Resilience is a powerful internal mechanism that empowers individuals to navigate the storms of life, enabling them to persevere through difficulties and maintain a sense of hope even in challenging circumstances. This quality allows people to adapt to adversity, transforming potential failures into stepping stones for future success. Rather than being defined by their setbacks, resilient individuals view challenges as opportunities for growth, using them as catalysts for change. Each obstacle faced becomes a lesson learned, contributing to a deeper understanding of themselves and the world around them. This mindset fosters a belief in one's abilities, reinforcing the idea that progress is possible and achievable even in the face of adversity.

Building resilience is integral to personal growth and self-confidence. It invites individuals to confront their fears and develop coping strategies that will serve them throughout life. By actively overcoming setbacks, individuals cultivate emotional strength, allowing them to face future challenges with greater assurance. Each experience of bouncing back not only enhances self-efficacy but also fosters a sense of community, as people often find support and connection through shared struggles. Resilience equips individuals with the tools necessary for transformation, enabling them to emerge from hardships intact, enriched, wiser, and ready to tackle whatever lies ahead with newfound confidence and determination.

Definition of Resilience

Resilience is the capacity to recover quickly from difficulties and adapt to challenging situations. It embodies a person's ability to withstand stress, overcome obstacles, and emerge from adversity with renewed strength and insight. Rather than a fixed trait, resilience can be developed and strengthened over time through experiences, attitudes, and behaviors that foster emotional flexibility and mental toughness. It encompasses various aspects, including emotional regulation, problem-solving skills, and a positive outlook, allowing individuals to navigate life's inevitable ups and downs with greater ease and confidence.

Importance of Resilience in Daily Life

Resilience plays a vital role in our daily lives, influencing how we respond to stressors, challenges, and unexpected changes. In both personal and professional contexts, resilient individuals are better equipped to cope with setbacks, maintaining their focus and motivation even in difficult circumstances. This ability enhances emotional well-being and promotes healthier relationships, as resilient people tend to exhibit empathy, understanding, and patience towards others. By fostering resilience, we can cultivate a proactive mindset, enabling us to approach challenges with curiosity and creativity rather than fear and avoidance. Ultimately, resilience empowers us to thrive in the face of adversity, leading to a more fulfilling and meaningful life.

Setbacks can be:

- An unavoidable part of the human experience.

- Manifesting in various forms, such as personal losses.

- Professional failures.

- Health issues.

- Unexpected life changes.

These challenges can evoke a wide range of emotions, including frustration, sadness, and anxiety, often leading individuals to feel overwhelmed or defeated. The impact of setbacks can extend beyond immediate feelings of distress; they can also disrupt routines, erode self-esteem, and create a sense of uncertainty about the future. However, it is essential to recognize that setbacks can also serve as powerful learning opportunities, prompting personal growth and deeper self-reflection. By understanding and embracing these challenges, individuals can harness their resilience, transforming adversity into a pathway for growth and empowerment.

Characteristics of Resilient Individuals

1. **Adaptability**: Resilient individuals are highly adaptable and flexible in their thinking and actions. They can adjust their strategies and approaches in response to changing circumstances, allowing them to navigate obstacles more effectively. This adaptability enables them to pivot when faced with setbacks rather than becoming stuck or overwhelmed.

2. **Optimism**: A positive outlook is a hallmark of resilience. Resilient individuals maintain hope and believe in their ability to overcome challenges. This optimism helps them see setbacks as temporary and surmountable, encouraging them to pursue solutions rather than dwell on problems. Their belief in a better future fuels their perseverance and motivates them to keep moving forward.

3. **Emotional Regulation**: Resilient individuals possess strong emotional intelligence, which allows them to recognize and manage their emotions effectively. They are aware of their feelings and can express them appropriately without being overwhelmed by them. This ability to regulate emotions helps them maintain focus and composure during difficult times.

4. **Problem-Solving Skills**: Resilient individuals are often skilled problem solvers. They approach challenges with a constructive mindset, analyzing situations to identify potential solutions. Rather than feeling helpless in the face of adversity, they take proactive steps to address issues, which reinforces their sense of control and agency.

5. **Strong Social Support**: Resilient individuals understand the importance of building and maintaining strong relationships. They actively seek support from friends, family, and colleagues, recognizing that connection can provide comfort and encouragement during tough times. This network of support helps them feel less isolated and more empowered to face challenges.

6. **Self-Confidence**: Another key characteristic of resilient individuals is a sense of self-efficacy. They believe in their abilities to handle challenges and are willing to take risks in pursuit of their goals. This self-confidence is reinforced by their past experiences of overcoming difficulties, fostering a belief that they can navigate future obstacles as well.

7. **Persistence**: Resilient individuals exhibit a strong sense of persistence and determination. They are willing to push through challenges and setbacks without giving up easily. This perseverance is often fueled by their goals and values, driving them to continue striving for success even when faced with adversity.

8. **Growth Mindset**: Resilient individuals often embrace a growth mindset, viewing failures and setbacks as opportunities for learning and development. They are open to feedback and are willing to reflect on their experiences to identify lessons that can inform their future actions. This perspective fosters continuous personal growth and reinforces their resilience over time.

The Influence of Beliefs and Mindsets on Resilience

Beliefs and mindsets are crucial in shaping our resilience and influencing how we perceive challenges, approach obstacles, and engage with the world. Resilience is not merely the ability to bounce back from setbacks but also the capacity to adapt, grow, and thrive in the face of adversity. By understanding how our beliefs and mindsets affect our behavior, we can harness the power of our brains to create lasting change and empowerment.

Beliefs and Resilience

Beliefs are deeply rooted perceptions we accept as true, often without questioning their validity. These beliefs shape our identity, influence our actions, and define what we think is possible or achievable. For instance, if an individual believes that they are inherently incompetent, this belief can become a self-fulfilling prophecy, leading to a lack of effort and motivation in the face of challenges. This perception limits their willingness to take risks and distorts their understanding of their potential for success.

Limiting beliefs, such as self-doubt and negative self-talk, can create significant barriers to resilience. They prevent us from seizing opportunities for growth and success, eroding our confidence and diminishing our motivation. When faced with challenges, these beliefs may lead us to avoid risks, retreat into our comfort zones, or even sabotage our own efforts. Such behaviors are counterproductive and can perpetuate a cycle of negative thinking that reinforces our limiting beliefs.

Overcoming these limiting beliefs requires self-awareness and introspection. It begins with recognizing and acknowledging these thoughts as they arise, allowing us to question their validity. Are these beliefs based on facts or rooted in fear, past failures, or external influences? By challenging these perceptions, we can transform them into empowering beliefs that affirm our abilities, encourage growth, and foster resilience. For example, replacing "I can't do this" with "I can learn how to do this" opens the door to possibility and encourages a proactive approach to challenges.

Mindset and Resilience

Mindset is a powerful determinant of behavior and resilience. It influences how we perceive challenges, handle obstacles, and interact with our environment. Mindset's power lies in its ability to shape our perceptions and behaviors, freeing us from limiting beliefs and allowing us to embrace growth, resilience, and empowerment.

A growth mindset, in particular, promotes resilience, adaptability, and a willingness to take risks and learn from mistakes. This concept, popularized by psychologist Carol Dweck, suggests that individuals with a growth mindset view their abilities as malleable rather than fixed. They believe that dedication and hard work can develop intelligence, talent, and skills. This perspective encourages individuals to approach challenges with curiosity and determination, seeing them as opportunities for growth rather than threats. When we cultivate a growth mindset, we are more likely to embrace setbacks as valuable learning experiences rather than insurmountable obstacles. This perspective fosters more adaptive and resilient approaches to life's challenges. For instance, if a person fails at a task, a growth mindset prompts them to analyze what went wrong, seek feedback, and adjust their strategy rather than dwelling on feelings of inadequacy. This proactive response helps individuals recover more quickly and builds a stronger foundation for future success.

Furthermore, adopting a growth mindset fosters a culture of resilience in collective environments, such as teams or communities. When individuals within a group share a belief in the power of growth and development, they support one another in overcoming challenges, enhancing overall resilience. This communal reinforcement can create a positive feedback loop where collective learning and shared experiences lead to greater adaptability and strength in the face of adversity.

Building Resilience

Building resilience requires self-awareness, commitment, and a willingness to challenge deeply rooted perceptions. By understanding the impact of beliefs and mindsets on our behavior, we can harness the power of our brain to create lasting change and build a life of empowerment.

Cultivating a Growth Mindset

Cultivating a growth mindset is essential for building resilience. With a growth mindset, we approach challenges with curiosity and determination, viewing them as opportunities for learning and development. Here are several strategies to help cultivate a growth mindset:

- Challenge Limiting Beliefs: Identify limiting beliefs about your abilities and potential. Question their validity and explore alternative perspectives that align with a growth mindset.

- Embrace Challenges: Approach challenges with an open mind, seeing them as opportunities for growth. Focus on the process of learning, valuing effort and persistence over immediate results.

- Learn from Mistakes: Treat mistakes as stepping stones to success. Reflect on what you can learn from setbacks, using those lessons to inform future decisions and actions.

- Foster Curiosity: Cultivate curiosity by exploring new ideas and experiences. Embrace diverse perspectives to broaden your understanding and creativity, using these insights to fuel personal growth.

Developing Adaptive Coping Strategies

Adaptive coping strategies are a key component of resilience. They allow us to manage stress, overcome challenges, and maintain emotional balance. Developing effective coping strategies equips us to face adversity with greater confidence and composure. Some strategies include:

- Mindfulness and Stress Management: Mindfulness practices, such as meditation and deep breathing, can help manage stress and improve emotional regulation. These practices create space for self-awareness and reflection, allowing us to respond thoughtfully rather than react impulsively to challenges.

- Problem-Solving Skills: Cultivating strong problem-solving skills enables us to approach obstacles with a clear, solutions-oriented mindset. Break down challenges into manageable steps, brainstorm potential solutions, and take action with confidence.

- Support Systems: Building a reliable support network of friends, family, and mentors provides emotional support and guidance during difficult times. Seeking advice or simply sharing your experiences with others can offer valuable perspective and encouragement.

- Physical Self-Care: Resilience is not solely a mental or emotional trait—it also involves taking care of our physical well-being. Regular exercise, a balanced diet, and adequate sleep are foundational to maintaining the energy and focus needed to face challenges.

Harnessing the Power of Resilience

Resilience empowers us to continue pursuing our goals despite setbacks and challenges. It is the foundation of personal growth, helping us adapt to change, overcome adversity, and emerge stronger. By cultivating resilience and a growth mindset, we can break free from limiting beliefs and embrace a life that aligns with our values and aspirations.

As you build resilience, remember that setbacks are not failures—they are opportunities for learning and transformation. By approaching challenges with an open mind, embracing effort over outcome, and developing adaptive coping strategies, you will foster personal growth and build a life of fulfillment and success.

Creating a balanced and fulfilling life requires adopting adaptive coping strategies that foster personal and collective growth. By integrating these strategies into our daily routine, we can navigate life's challenges with resilience and maintain emotional well-being.

One powerful approach is through mindfulness and meditation. Mindfulness practices cultivate awareness, presence, and emotional regulation, helping us stay grounded even in stressful situations. Techniques such as deep breathing, body scanning, and guided meditation allow us to manage stress more effectively and maintain emotional balance.

Another key strategy is practicing self-compassion and self-care. Prioritizing our well-being is essential during times of stress and adversity. Treating ourselves with kindness and understanding, especially when things get tough, helps us to recharge and avoid burnout. Incorporating regular self-care routines can enhance emotional and physical health, providing a foundation of resilience.

Incorporating gratitude and positive psychology is equally transformative. By focusing on the positive aspects of our lives, we can shift our mindset toward appreciation and optimism. Acknowledging our strengths, accomplishments, and potential allows us to build a mindset that encourages personal growth and fulfillment.

Overcoming Setbacks

Setbacks are an inevitable part of life, but overcoming them is an essential aspect of building resilience. Setbacks provide opportunities for growth, and by changing our mindset and beliefs, we can harness the power of these experiences to create lasting change.

One effective approach is embracing setbacks as opportunities for growth. Reframing setbacks as valuable learning experiences allows us to extract lessons from adversity and apply them to future challenges. Reflecting on setbacks can inform future actions, inspiring new approaches and strategies that lead to success. Additionally, using adaptive coping strategies to handle stress and adversity is crucial. Focusing on problem-solving and emotional regulation enables us to approach setbacks with a solution-oriented mindset. This proactive attitude fosters resilience and determination, helping us overcome challenges with confidence.

Cultivating resilience itself is a key factor in handling setbacks. A positive mindset, combined with adaptive coping strategies, enables us to approach challenges as opportunities for learning and growth. By embracing setbacks, we become more capable of facing future difficulties with greater ease.

Building a Supportive Network

A supportive network plays an important role in overcoming setbacks. Having a group of people who encourage and uplift us can provide strength, guidance, and accountability as we navigate life's obstacles.

To build such a network, it's essential to seek support from friends, family, and mentors who can offer advice and emotional support. Surrounding ourselves with people who believe in our potential can make a significant difference during tough times. Additionally, building connections with like-minded individuals who share similar values and aspirations helps foster a sense of community. These relationships provide mutual support and inspiration, reinforcing our personal growth journey.

Engaging in community activities and initiatives that align with our values can further enhance our sense of belonging and contribute to collective growth. When we actively participate in communities that resonate with our goals, we not only build support but also contribute to a shared vision of empowerment and progress.

The Path Forward

Resilience is a powerful, transformative force that shapes both our individual lives and the world around us. By understanding how beliefs and mindset influence our behavior, we can unlock the potential to overcome limiting beliefs, build resilience, and achieve our goals. This journey requires courage, commitment, and a willingness to confront the beliefs that no longer serve us.

As we move forward, it is essential to cultivate self-awareness, compassion, and resilience. By embracing our authentic selves and reframing our limiting beliefs, we can create a life that aligns with our values and aspirations. The path to empowerment is a continuous process—one that offers limitless possibilities for personal growth and collective evolution.

In the next chapter, we will explore how to embrace empowering beliefs and examine the profound impact of mindset on our actions. You will be equipped with practical tools and techniques to align your life with your deepest values. Through self-awareness, introspection, and a commitment to growth, you will unlock your potential and confidently step onto the path to empowerment.

CHAPTER EIGHT

EMBRACING EMPOWERING BELIEFS

Empowering beliefs are the foundation of personal growth, providing the mindset and tools for change, learning, and development. These deep-rooted perceptions affirm our worth, potential, and ability to achieve our goals. By adopting empowering beliefs, we open ourselves to opportunities for success and transformation, creating a life that aligns with our values and aspirations. They shape how we see ourselves, the world around us, and the possibilities that lie ahead. While limiting beliefs hold us back, keeping us trapped in cycles of fear, self-doubt, and inaction, empowering beliefs do the opposite. They open doors, instill confidence, and propel us forward toward our goals and dreams. Embracing empowering beliefs is a transformative process that shifts our perspective from seeing obstacles to recognizing growth opportunities.

Our beliefs act as a lens through which we interpret our experiences and define what is possible. When we adopt empowering beliefs, we equip ourselves with the mental and emotional tools to navigate challenges, bounce back from setbacks, and seize opportunities. These beliefs are not just feel-good thoughts—they are actionable perspectives that shape our decisions, relationships, and the overall quality of our lives.

Understanding Empowering Beliefs

Empowering beliefs are deeply rooted perceptions affirming our capabilities and potential as a foundation for navigating life's challenges and opportunities. These core beliefs shape not only how we see ourselves but also how we perceive the world around us. Adopting empowering beliefs influences our behavior, guiding our actions and decisions to align with our values and goals. Empowering beliefs create a mindset that fuels success and personal development by fostering self-confidence, resilience, and positive self-talk.

One of the most significant impacts of empowering beliefs is how they shape our self-image. When we believe in our abilities, we are more likely to take risks, seize opportunities, and step outside our comfort zones. This self-assurance creates a mental framework that supports our goals and motivates us to take consistent action. For example, if we believe that we can learn new skills, we are more inclined to embrace challenges with curiosity rather than fear. This confidence drives our ambition and allows us to handle setbacks with grace and perseverance.

Empowering beliefs are deeply connected to our personal values and aspirations because they reflect what we truly stand for and what we hope to achieve in life. Unlike limiting beliefs, which often create inner conflict by undermining our desires, empowering beliefs serve as a foundation for aligning our actions and decisions with our core values. When our beliefs support our values, we experience greater clarity, motivation, and purpose in our daily lives.

For example, if one of your core values is personal growth, adopting an empowering belief such as "I am capable of learning and improving" will naturally propel you toward opportunities that foster development. This alignment helps you stay focused on your goals and maintain resilience in the face of challenges because your belief system supports your long-term aspirations. It encourages a mindset of growth and adaptability, making it easier to embrace change and pursue new opportunities.

Empowering beliefs also foster resilience, enabling us to view obstacles as temporary roadblocks rather than insurmountable barriers. Instead of seeing setbacks as reflections of personal failure, individuals with empowering beliefs perceive them as opportunities for growth. This shift in perspective is crucial for maintaining motivation and focus during difficult times. By reframing challenges as learning experiences, we can extract valuable lessons that help us improve and adapt. This continuous learning and self-improvement process is at the heart of personal growth and development.

It fuels positive self-talk, which is essential for maintaining a healthy mindset. Our inner dialogue becomes encouraging and supportive when we internalize positive beliefs about ourselves. This positive self-talk acts as a buffer against self-doubt and negative thinking, reinforcing our belief in our ability to overcome difficulties. For instance, when faced with a daunting task, someone with empowering beliefs might think, "I can figure this out," or "I have the skills to succeed." This internal reinforcement creates a mental environment where confidence thrives, allowing us to approach challenges with determination and optimism.

Empowering beliefs encourage us to pursue opportunities with confidence. When we believe in our potential, we are more likely to recognize and act on opportunities that align with our aspirations. This proactive mindset allows us to take calculated risks, innovate, and explore new possibilities, all contributing to personal and professional growth. Empowering beliefs give us the courage to push boundaries, knowing that even if we encounter setbacks, we have the strength and resilience to persevere. Moreover, empowering beliefs help bridge the gap between where you are now and where you want to be. They provide the confidence and clarity needed to pursue meaningful aspirations in your career, relationships, or personal development. By cultivating beliefs that reflect your potential, you're better equipped to take risks, overcome obstacles, and achieve goals that are aligned with your authentic self and long-term vision for your life.

Characteristics of Empowering Beliefs

1. Positive and Constructive: Empowering beliefs focus on strengths and possibilities, encouraging progress rather than limitations.

2. Aligned with Reality: These beliefs are based on realistic assessments, grounded in evidence and facts.

3. Growth-Oriented: Empowering beliefs support learning, improvement, and embracing challenges for personal development.

4. Self-Compassionate: They encourage kindness towards oneself, especially in the face of mistakes or setbacks.

5. Action-Oriented: These beliefs motivate proactive behavior and the pursuit of goals.

6. Flexible and Adaptable: Empowering beliefs can evolve with new experiences and information, allowing for change.

7. Focused on Possibilities, Not Limits: They emphasize opportunities and potential rather than dwelling on obstacles or failures.

The Influence of Beliefs and Mindset on Empowerment

Beliefs and mindset are foundational in shaping how we experience empowerment. They influence how we perceive challenges, respond to obstacles, and engage with the world around us. Our beliefs and mindset serve as mental filters, influencing every decision we make and shaping our capacity for growth and achievement. By understanding the profound influence of these internal dynamics, we can actively harness the power of our minds to create lasting, transformative change.

Beliefs and Empowerment

Beliefs are deeply ingrained perceptions that we accept as truths, often without questioning their validity. These beliefs form the core of our identity, influencing how we view ourselves, our potential, and the possibilities available to us. When we internalize limiting beliefs, such as "I'm not good enough" or "I'll never succeed," these negative perceptions can become self-fulfilling prophecies, holding us back from pursuing our goals and realizing our full potential. They create mental barriers that prevent us from stepping into our power and taking the necessary risks to grow and succeed.

On the other hand, empowering beliefs create a mental framework that fosters confidence, motivation, and resilience. When we hold beliefs such as "I am capable," "I can learn and grow," or "Challenges are opportunities," we create an internal environment that nurtures our potential. Empowering beliefs allow us to approach life with a mindset of possibility, fostering the courage to take on challenges, explore new opportunities, and persevere in the face of adversity. These beliefs shape how we see ourselves and the world, and they fuel the drive to pursue growth, embrace uncertainty, and make decisions that align with our values and aspirations.

Importantly, empowering beliefs are not fixed—they can be cultivated and strengthened over time. The process of challenging and reframing limiting beliefs into empowering ones is essential for personal growth. By consciously examining and altering the beliefs that limit us, we can create a mental framework that supports our ambitions, encouraging us to step into our full potential with confidence and determination. As we do this, we set the stage for greater empowerment, enabling us to take control of our lives and shape our future in meaningful ways.

Mindset and Empowerment

Mindset is another powerful driver of behavior, significantly impacting how we navigate life's challenges and opportunities. At its core, mindset refers to our beliefs and attitudes about ourselves, our abilities, and the world around us. It dictates how we view challenges, cope with difficulties, and interpret success and failure. A fixed mindset is characterized by the belief that our abilities and intelligence are static and unchangeable. Individuals with a fixed mindset often see challenges as threats to their self-worth, leading to avoidance behaviors, fear of failure, and an unwillingness to take risks.

In contrast, a growth mindset is based on the belief that abilities and intelligence can be developed through effort, learning, and perseverance. People with a growth mindset view challenges as opportunities for growth rather than threats to their identity. They are more likely to take risks, learn from mistakes, and persist in the face of difficulties. This mindset fosters resilience and adaptability, key components of empowerment. When we approach life with a growth mindset, we are better equipped to overcome setbacks, continuously improve, and achieve our goals.

A growth mindset empowers us by breaking the mental chains of limiting beliefs. It encourages us to embrace challenges with curiosity and determination, seeing them as opportunities for learning and self-improvement rather than obstacles to success. This mindset is essential for empowerment because it fosters an openness to new experiences, the willingness to evolve, and the courage to take risks—all of which are necessary for personal and professional growth.

When we cultivate a growth mindset, we empower ourselves to continuously seek out development opportunities, regardless of the challenges we may face. This perspective allows us to approach life with greater resilience and adaptability, ensuring that we are better equipped to handle life's uncertainties and setbacks. The willingness to learn from mistakes and persist despite adversity is what fuels both personal and collective growth. It empowers us to lead lives that are aligned with our values and aspirations, creating a sense of fulfillment and purpose.

The Synergy Between Beliefs and Mindset

Beliefs and mindsets create a powerful synergy that influences every aspect of our lives. Our beliefs shape our mindset, and our mindset, in turn, shapes our behavior. When we cultivate empowering beliefs and adopt a growth mindset, we create a positive feedback loop that reinforces our ability to overcome challenges, seize opportunities, and confidently pursue our goals. This dynamic combination fuels our journey toward empowerment, enabling us to take control of our lives and unlock our full potential.

The influence of beliefs and mindset on empowerment cannot be overstated. By examining and transforming limiting beliefs, we create a mental framework that supports growth, resilience, and success. By cultivating a growth mindset, we develop the tools and attitudes necessary to navigate challenges, learn from mistakes, and continuously evolve. Together, these internal dynamics form the foundation of empowerment, allowing us to live fulfilling, purpose-driven lives and to inspire others to do the same.

Embracing Empowering Beliefs

Adopting empowering beliefs requires self-awareness, commitment, and a willingness to challenge long-held perceptions. By examining our beliefs and understanding how they shape our behavior, we can begin to shift our mindset and create lasting empowerment.

Cultivating Empowering Beliefs

To fully embrace empowerment, we must cultivate empowering beliefs that support our goals and aspirations. These beliefs allow us to view challenges as opportunities for growth and approach life with a sense of determination.

Consider the following strategies to cultivate empowering beliefs:

- Challenge Limiting Beliefs: Identify limiting beliefs about your abilities and potential, and question their validity. Replace them with empowering perspectives that align with your values and goals.

- Embrace Positive Self-Talk: Focus on your strengths, accomplishments, and growth potential. Use positive affirmations to reinforce your belief in yourself.

- Reinforce Empowering Beliefs: Strengthen your empowering beliefs through consistent practice. Incorporate positive self-talk, visualization, and gratitude exercises to solidify these beliefs and create lasting change.

Building Confidence and Self-Esteem

Confidence and self-esteem are integral components of empowerment. They enable you to pursue opportunities for growth and success with determination. Building confidence requires a focus on your strengths and a commitment to reinforcing empowering beliefs.

To build your confidence and self-esteem, consider these strategies:

- Set Achievable Goals: Break down larger goals into manageable steps and celebrate each accomplishment. This will help reinforce your belief in your abilities.

- Recognize Your Strengths: Reflect on your past successes and the strengths that contributed to them. Use this awareness to build confidence in your future endeavors.

- Practice Self-Compassion: Treat yourself with kindness and understanding when facing setbacks. Embrace mistakes as part of the learning process and an opportunity for growth.

The Path Forward: Empowering Beliefs in Action

Empowering beliefs have the ability to shape your reality and unlock your potential. By adopting a growth mindset and cultivating beliefs that affirm your worth and abilities, you create a foundation for lifelong success and fulfillment. This process requires consistent effort, self-reflection, and a commitment to challenging and reframing limiting beliefs.

As you move forward, remember that empowerment is an ongoing journey. By reinforcing positive beliefs, embracing opportunities for growth, and building resilience, you can create a life aligned with your values and aspirations.

Celebrating your successes and achievements is a vital part of personal growth. By acknowledging the value of your efforts and perseverance, you reinforce the belief in your ability to accomplish great things. Each success, whether big or small, serves as motivation to continue pursuing your goals and aspirations. Taking the time to reflect on and celebrate these victories not only builds self-confidence but also energizes you to tackle the next challenge with renewed vigor.

Show Self-Compassion

Practicing self-compassion is essential, particularly during times of stress and adversity. When you prioritize your well-being and approach yourself with kindness and understanding, you build a strong foundation for emotional resilience. Self-compassion allows you to treat yourself with the same empathy you would extend to a loved one. Instead of being overly critical, it encourages you to recognize that everyone faces setbacks and moments of struggle. By embracing this mindset, you can recover from challenges more gracefully, fostering a healthier and more supportive relationship with yourself. This approach not only aids in overcoming difficulties but also helps in developing the emotional strength needed to navigate life's ups and downs.

Incorporating self-care and mindfulness practices into your daily routine can reinforce self-compassion. Acknowledge that setbacks are part of the growth process, not a reflection of personal failure. By allowing yourself to feel vulnerable and imperfect without judgment, you cultivate a mindset rooted in patience and acceptance. This shift in perspective enables continuous progress, as you are more likely to view challenges as opportunities for growth rather than insurmountable obstacles. Ultimately, self-compassion is a powerful tool for nurturing emotional well-being, self-awareness, and long-term personal development.

Cultivate Gratitude

Gratitude is an incredibly powerful tool for personal development and emotional well-being. When you take the time to reflect on the positive aspects of your life—whether it's your strengths, achievements, or simply the everyday blessings—you shift your mindset from scarcity to abundance. This shift encourages a more positive outlook on life and helps you approach challenges with optimism rather than fear. By regularly practicing gratitude, you begin to focus on what you have achieved and how far you've come, which boosts your confidence and motivation. This practice also fosters resilience, as it helps you reframe difficulties as temporary and manageable rather than overwhelming.

Beyond improving your mood and outlook, cultivating gratitude strengthens your sense of purpose. Recognizing the progress you've made and the good in your life fosters a mindset that attracts further success and fulfillment. Gratitude also deepens your appreciation for the present moment and helps you stay grounded, even when faced with adversity. By celebrating both small and large victories, you reinforce positive beliefs about your capabilities, which fuels ongoing growth and development. This practice not only improves your emotional well-being but also promotes a healthier, more fulfilling life trajectory.

The Impact of Self-Confidence Beliefs on Personal Growth

Strengthening your beliefs has a profound impact on personal growth. It influences your ability to pursue goals, overcome challenges, and find fulfillment in life. Adopting empowering beliefs allows you to align your actions with your values and aspirations, fostering resilience, empowerment, and a sense of achievement. When you believe in your potential, you open the door to endless possibilities for growth and success.

Pursuing Your Goals and Aspirations

Strengthening your beliefs empowers you to pursue your goals and aspirations with confidence and determination. Adopting a growth mindset helps you overcome limiting beliefs and self-doubt, making it easier to seize opportunities for personal and professional growth. By focusing on progress and development rather than perfection, you can approach your goals with a sense of curiosity and resilience.

To pursue your goals with empowering beliefs, consider these strategies:

- **Set growth-minded goals:** Establish goals that align with your values and aspirations, focusing on continuous growth rather than mere performance. Use these goals as a roadmap for personal development.
- **Embrace the learning process:** Value effort and perseverance over immediate success. Approach your goals with an open mind, seeing setbacks as valuable opportunities for learning and improvement.
- **Celebrate progress:** Acknowledge and celebrate your progress, understanding that every step forward is an achievement. Use each success as motivation to continue striving toward your goals.

Overcoming Challenges and Setbacks

Strengthening your beliefs equips you to handle challenges and setbacks with resilience and adaptability. A growth-oriented mindset enables you to see difficulties as stepping stones for growth rather than insurmountable barriers. By reframing challenges as opportunities for learning, you can use them to inform your future actions and fuel your personal growth.

Here are some strategies for overcoming challenges with powerful beliefs:

- **Embrace change and uncertainty:** View change and uncertainty as opportunities for growth. Use these moments to deepen your understanding of the world and your place within it.
- **Use adaptive coping strategies:** Employ problem-solving and emotion regulation techniques to manage stress and adversity effectively.
- **Promote resilience:** Cultivate a positive mindset that encourages resilience. Use each setback as an opportunity to learn and grow, approaching challenges with confidence and determination.

Future Directions

The power of strengthening beliefs is a transformative force that can shape your life and the world around you. By understanding the impact your beliefs and mindset have on your behavior, you can harness this power to overcome limiting beliefs, build resilience, and achieve your goals. This journey requires courage, commitment, and a willingness to confront the beliefs that no longer serve you.

As you embark on this journey, it is crucial to cultivate self-awareness, compassion, and resilience. By embracing your true self and reframing your beliefs, you can create a life that is aligned with your values and aspirations. The path to self-empowerment is a continuous process of learning, growth, and transformation, offering endless opportunities for personal and collective advancement.

In the next chapters, we will explore how to build a supportive environment, delve into how beliefs and mindsets shape behavior, and equip ourselves with practical tools and techniques for creating a life that aligns with our values and aspirations. Through self-awareness, introspection, and a commitment to growth, you will unlock your potential and begin your journey toward self-empowerment.

CHAPTER NINE

CREATING A SUPPORTIVE ENVIRONMENT

Creating a supportive environment is vital for personal growth and empowerment, as it serves as the foundation for positive change, learning, and development. Such an environment nurtures a sense of safety and encouragement, allowing you to explore new ideas and push past your limitations without fear of judgment or failure. This space promotes self-reflection, growth, and continuous learning by surrounding you with individuals who uplift and inspire you. It offers opportunities to share experiences, exchange knowledge, and receive constructive feedback, all of which contribute to the development of self-confidence and a growth-oriented mindset. With the right environment, you are more likely to take calculated risks and embrace challenges, knowing that you have the support to succeed and grow.

A supportive environment boosts motivation and determination, providing the emotional and mental resources necessary to pursue your goals. It acts as a catalyst for resilience, helping you overcome obstacles and setbacks with the belief that you are capable of achieving your aspirations. When you are surrounded by encouragement, it becomes easier to stay focused on your vision and maintain momentum, even during difficult times. Ultimately, this environment aligns with your values and aspirations, fostering both personal and collective growth, and enabling you to move toward your dreams with purpose and confidence.

Understanding the Importance of a Supportive Environment

A supportive environment is an essential foundation for personal growth, resilience, and empowerment. It creates a nurturing space where individuals can feel safe, understood, and motivated to pursue their aspirations. This environment doesn't happen by chance; it requires intentional effort to cultivate and sustain. When surrounded by positivity—through relationships, communities, or personal habits—we build an atmosphere that fosters exploration, learning, and risk-taking. This sense of support enables us to step outside our comfort zones and embrace challenges, knowing that we have a strong network to lean on when difficulties arise. The encouragement and reinforcement from this environment strengthen our self-confidence and empower us to pursue our goals with determination.

One of the key benefits of a supportive environment is its impact on emotional well-being. It provides emotional security, allowing individuals to maintain balance and manage stress more effectively. When we feel supported, we are better equipped to navigate life's inevitable ups and downs without becoming overwhelmed. Positive reinforcement from those around us serves as a buffer against the stresses of daily life, reducing feelings of isolation and anxiety. Whether it's receiving encouragement from family, guidance from mentors, or simply the presence of friends who listen and empathize, this kind of environment creates the emotional stability necessary for personal growth and development.

A supportive environment also plays a crucial role in fostering resilience. Resilience is the ability to bounce back from setbacks and adapt to change, and it is greatly influenced by the people and resources around us. When faced with adversity, having a network of supportive individuals or resources can be the difference between giving up and persevering. This environment not only helps us handle challenges more effectively but also encourages us to see setbacks as opportunities for growth. The presence of positive influences reinforces the belief that we are capable of overcoming difficulties, and this confidence fuels our resilience, pushing us to keep striving toward our goals.

Furthermore, a supportive environment promotes a growth mindset, which is essential for long-term success. A growth mindset encourages us to view challenges as learning opportunities rather than threats. When surrounded by people who reinforce this mindset, we are more likely to embrace challenges, take calculated risks, and learn from our mistakes. This environment fosters a sense of curiosity and determination, motivating us to continuously improve and evolve. By surrounding ourselves with influences that promote learning and personal development, we create a dynamic space where growth becomes a natural part of our daily lives.

In the long run, cultivating a supportive environment has lasting effects on both personal and collective development. It strengthens our ability to maintain focus on our aspirations, builds resilience, and enhances emotional well-being. By creating and nurturing an environment that promotes positivity, learning, and encouragement, we not only benefit ourselves but also contribute to the growth of those around us. The mutual reinforcement of support and empowerment creates a cycle of success, where individuals are inspired to pursue their goals with confidence and perseverance. Ultimately, this environment aligns with our values and aspirations, allowing us to live a more fulfilling and purposeful life.

The Influence of Beliefs and Mindsets on a Supportive Environment

Beliefs and mindsets play a critical role in shaping the supportive environment we create for ourselves. They influence how we perceive challenges, approach obstacles, and engage with the world. By understanding how beliefs and mindsets affect our behavior, we can harness their power to create lasting change and personal empowerment.

Beliefs and a Supportive Environment

Beliefs are powerful mental constructs that significantly influence how we perceive the world and ourselves. These deeply ingrained perceptions often go unquestioned, forming the foundation for our decisions, actions, and the environments we cultivate. Limiting beliefs—such as self-doubt, fear of failure, or feelings of inadequacy—are particularly detrimental, as they create mental and emotional barriers that hinder personal progress. For instance, when we believe that we're not good enough or fear taking risks, we limit our ability to seize opportunities that could propel us toward our potential. These limiting beliefs not only affect our actions but also the environments we build around us, often leading to stagnation and reinforcing a cycle of inaction and self-sabotage.

On the other hand, empowering beliefs act as catalysts for personal growth and success. Beliefs rooted in self-confidence, optimism, and a sense of capability fuel motivation and determination. They encourage us to take risks, embrace challenges, and maintain resilience when faced with adversity. These beliefs form a mental framework that actively supports our goals and aspirations, creating an internal environment where success feels attainable. When we believe in our potential and our ability to learn and grow, we approach life with a mindset that is open to possibilities. This shift in perspective allows us to move forward with curiosity, explore new paths, and develop a resilience that propels us even in the face of challenges.

A supportive environment, whether internal or external, plays a key role in nurturing empowering beliefs. It reinforces positive self-perceptions, creating the conditions necessary for these beliefs to flourish and guide us toward success. Internally, a supportive environment includes practices like self-reflection, self-compassion, and intentional goal-setting, which align our mindset with our aspirations. Externally, it involves surrounding ourselves with positive influences, including relationships, mentors, and resources that encourage growth. When the environment around us is supportive, it continually validates and strengthens the empowering beliefs we cultivate, allowing us to stay motivated and focused on our long-term goals.

The interaction between beliefs and a supportive environment is reciprocal. As we foster empowering beliefs, we naturally begin to shape our surroundings to reflect this new outlook. We seek out people who encourage and uplift us, choose environments that challenge us to grow, and engage in activities that align with our values and aspirations. This positive feedback loop creates a synergy where empowering beliefs and a nurturing environment feed into each other, enabling us to pursue personal and professional growth with renewed energy and commitment. The beliefs we hold and the environments we cultivate are intertwined. By identifying and transforming limiting beliefs, and actively creating spaces—both mental and physical—that nurture positive growth, we can unlock our full potential. Empowering beliefs, supported by a nurturing environment, act as the cornerstone of personal development, enabling us to not only pursue our dreams but also to create a life of fulfillment, resilience, and success.

Mindset and a Supportive Environment

Mindset significantly influences how we approach challenges and opportunities, shaping our behavior and the environment we create. A growth mindset views failures as learning opportunities and encourages us to embrace challenges for personal and professional development. In contrast, a fixed mindset limits growth by seeing abilities as unchangeable and avoiding risks, which leads to stagnation and missed opportunities. The good news is that mindset can be shifted. By cultivating a growth mindset through reframing negative thoughts, seeking feedback, and embracing challenges, we can create an environment that promotes continuous learning and self-improvement. This mindset shift empowers us to face obstacles with confidence, recognizing each challenge as a step toward progress.

In a supportive environment fostered by a growth mindset, failures become lessons, and successes are milestones of growth. This positive feedback loop between mindset and environment propels us toward greater fulfillment and achievement. Ultimately, aligning a growth mindset with a supportive environment unlocks our potential, enabling us to pursue meaningful goals with resilience and purpose.

Building a Supportive Environment

Creating a supportive environment requires intentional effort and a commitment to nurturing the right conditions for growth. Here are some key strategies to help you build an environment that fosters personal empowerment:

- **Surround Yourself with Positive Influences:** The people you surround yourself with can significantly impact your mindset and beliefs. Seek out relationships that uplift, encourage, and inspire you. A supportive network of friends, mentors, and colleagues can provide valuable feedback, offer new perspectives, and help you stay accountable to your goals.

- **Create Routines that Support Growth:** Establish daily practices that encourage personal development and reflection. Whether it's journaling, meditation, or setting aside time for self-care, these routines can help you stay focused on your goals and maintain emotional balance.

- **Cultivate a Growth Mindset:** Challenge limiting beliefs by adopting a growth mindset. Embrace challenges, view setbacks as learning opportunities, and remind yourself that improvement is always possible. This mindset shift will enhance your ability to persevere and achieve your aspirations.
- **Nurture Your Physical and Mental Well-Being:** A supportive environment also includes taking care of your physical and mental health. Prioritize exercise, healthy eating, and mental wellness practices that keep you energized and focused. When your body and mind are well-nourished, you'll have the strength to face challenges with confidence.

The Power of Beliefs and Mindsets

Ultimately, the power of beliefs and mindsets lies in their ability to shape our perceptions and behaviors. When we nurture a supportive environment, we give ourselves the space to challenge limiting beliefs and develop empowering ones. By doing so, we create a life filled with purpose, growth, and success.

We can free ourselves from limiting beliefs and embrace a life of growth, resilience, and self-determination. A growth mindset promotes adaptability, a willingness to take risks, and the ability to learn from mistakes. By cultivating this mindset, we approach challenges with curiosity and determination, seeing them as opportunities for development rather than obstacles. Adopting a growth mindset equips us with the resilience needed to navigate life's uncertainties, fostering both personal and collective progress.

Create a Supportive Environment

Creating a supportive environment is crucial for overcoming limiting beliefs and achieving empowerment. This process requires self-awareness, a commitment to personal growth, and a willingness to challenge deeply rooted perceptions. By understanding how our beliefs and mindsets influence our actions, we can harness the power of our brains to create lasting change. Building a nurturing environment around us accelerates this transformation, allowing us to grow with strength and determination.

Building a Support Network

A strong support network is essential for navigating challenges and achieving success. Having people who believe in your abilities and encourage your progress can make a significant difference in your journey toward personal growth. Consider these strategies to build a support network:

- **Seek support:** Surround yourself with friends, family, and mentors who encourage your growth, provide guidance, and hold you accountable.
- **Build connections:** Foster relationships with like-minded individuals who share your values and aspirations. This sense of community enhances your personal and collective growth.
- **Join a community:** Engage in activities or groups that align with your goals and values. Being part of a community can provide opportunities for learning, collaboration, and mutual support.

Creating a Positive Environment

In addition to a support network, a positive environment is key to fostering personal growth and success. When we create an atmosphere of positivity, we gain the confidence to pursue opportunities with determination. To cultivate a positive environment, consider the following strategies:

- **Promote positivity:** Focus on the positive aspects of your life and express gratitude for your strengths, achievements, and potential.
- **Remove negative thoughts:** Identify and challenge the negative beliefs and self-talk that undermine your confidence and motivation. Replace them with empowering thoughts.
- **Cultivate gratitude:** Regularly reflect on the good things in your life, acknowledging the progress you've made and expressing gratitude for your growth potential.

How a Supportive Environment Impacts Personal Growth

A supportive environment plays a pivotal role in fostering personal growth by providing the emotional and psychological foundation needed to thrive. When you are surrounded by individuals who believe in your abilities and encourage your efforts, it boosts your confidence and reinforces your belief in your potential. This positive reinforcement helps you take on challenges that might otherwise seem daunting, knowing that you have a safety net of encouragement to fall back on. In this way, a supportive environment nurtures resilience, empowering you to face setbacks with determination rather than discouragement. Moreover, such an environment creates space for self-reflection and growth by fostering open communication and understanding. When you're surrounded by positive influences—whether it's family, friends, mentors, or colleagues—you're more likely to receive constructive feedback and advice that pushes you toward self-improvement. This openness to learning from others helps you recognize areas for development, while also offering a sense of accountability to stay on track with your goals. As a result, personal development is not only encouraged but actively supported.

A supportive environment aligns with long-term fulfillment by promoting a sense of belonging and emotional well-being. When you feel understood, valued, and connected to those around you, it becomes easier to pursue goals that resonate with your authentic self. This alignment allows you to make choices that reflect your core values and aspirations, leading to sustained motivation and a sense of purpose. With the backing of a nurturing and positive environment, personal growth becomes an ongoing, fulfilling journey rather than a solitary or overwhelming endeavor.

Pursue Your Goals and Aspirations

A supportive environment helps you pursue your goals with confidence and clarity. By adopting a growth-oriented approach, you can overcome limiting beliefs and self-doubt, focusing on the opportunities that lead to success. To make the most of your goals and aspirations in a nurturing environment, try these strategies:

- **Set growth-oriented goals:** Establish goals aligned with your values and aspirations, prioritizing personal development over pure performance. These goals act as a guide for growth and achievement.
- **Embrace the learning process:** Focus on effort and perseverance, rather than just results. View setbacks and challenges as learning experiences that contribute to your growth.
- **Celebrate progress:** Recognize and celebrate your achievements, no matter how small. Acknowledge the value of effort and use success as motivation to continue striving toward your goals.

Overcoming Challenges and Setbacks

A supportive environment also provides the strength needed to face difficulties with resilience and adaptability. When challenges arise, a growth mindset helps you view setbacks as learning opportunities that inspire future actions. In a supportive setting, setbacks become stepping stones for growth rather than obstacles that hold you back. To overcome challenges in a positive environment, embrace the mindset that every difficulty carries valuable lessons that will guide your future success.

With the right support and mindset, you can overcome limiting beliefs, pursue your goals with passion, and grow in ways you never imagined possible.

Embracing change and uncertainty is a vital part of personal growth. Instead of fearing the unknown, we should view it as an opportunity to expand our understanding of the world and to grow as individuals. When we welcome change, we open ourselves up to new experiences that challenge our existing beliefs, push us beyond our comfort zones, and help us develop resilience. This mindset shift allows us to see uncertainty not as a threat but as a chance to improve, learn, and thrive.

In times of stress or adversity, using adaptive coping strategies is essential for managing emotions and finding solutions. By focusing on problem-solving and regulating our emotional responses, we can navigate difficult situations more effectively. Adaptive coping strategies help us remain calm and focused, even in the face of challenges. They encourage us to face problems head-on, rather than avoid them, fostering a sense of control and confidence in our ability to overcome obstacles.

Resilience is built by adopting a positive attitude toward setbacks and seeing them as opportunities for growth. When we approach challenges with confidence and determination, we transform difficult experiences into lessons that help us improve. Resilience enables us to bounce back from adversity, adapt to new circumstances, and continue moving forward with purpose. It is a skill that can be nurtured through practice, allowing us to face life's inevitable ups and downs with grace and strength.

Future Directions

The power of a supportive environment is transformative. It can shape not only our lives but the world around us. By understanding how our beliefs and mindsets influence our behavior, we can harness this power to overcome limiting beliefs, build resilience, and reach our full potential. This journey, however, requires courage, commitment, and the willingness to confront beliefs that no longer serve us.

As we embark on this path, cultivating self-awareness, compassion, and resilience is key. By embracing our true selves and reframing our limiting beliefs, we align our lives with our values and aspirations. The path to empowerment is not a one-time event but a continuous process of learning, growing, and transforming. It offers endless opportunities for both personal and collective development.

In the chapters to come, we will explore the ongoing journey of growth. We will delve into how our beliefs and mindsets influence our actions and provide practical tools and techniques for creating a life that is aligned with your deepest values and aspirations. Through self-awareness, introspection, and a commitment to growth, you will unlock your potential and begin the journey toward self-determination and lasting empowerment.

CHAPTER TEN

THE JOURNEY OF CONTINUOUS GROWTH

The journey of continuous growth is a dynamic and transformative process that extends far beyond traditional notions of achievement or success. It encapsulates the idea that personal development is not a destination but an ongoing journey characterized by exploration, learning, and self-discovery. Embracing this perspective allows individuals to cultivate resilience, adapt to change, and unlock their true potential. In an ever-evolving world, where challenges and opportunities abound, a commitment to continuous growth becomes essential for navigating life's complexities.

Central to this journey is the concept of a growth mindset—the belief that abilities and intelligence can be developed through dedication, effort, and perseverance. This mindset contrasts sharply with a fixed mindset, which limits potential by assuming that talents are innate and unchangeable. By adopting a growth mindset, individuals empower themselves to embrace challenges, learn from failures, and pursue opportunities aligned with their values and aspirations. This shift in thinking sets the stage for a lifelong commitment to growth, fostering a sense of purpose and fulfillment.

What is continuous Growth?

Continuous growth refers to the ongoing process of personal development, learning, and self-improvement throughout one's life. It embodies the idea that growth is not a one-time event or a series of isolated achievements but rather a dynamic and evolving journey. Continuous growth involves regularly challenging oneself, embracing new experiences, and adapting to changes in both personal and professional contexts.

Continuous growth is a lifelong journey of learning, transformation, and empowerment. It involves embracing change, pursuing opportunities for development, and seeking fulfillment in every aspect of life. This ongoing process of growth is essential for personal and collective empowerment, offering opportunities for transformation, learning, and continuous development.

Understanding Continuous Growth

Continuous growth is a multifaceted and evolving process that allows individuals to pursue their goals and aspirations with a sense of confidence and determination. Unlike static achievements, which can often lead to complacency, continuous growth is characterized by an ongoing journey of learning, development, and self-improvement. This process is not an inherent trait; instead, it is a skill that can be cultivated and strengthened through intentional practices, experiences, and a willingness to embrace new challenges. By adopting a mindset oriented towards continuous growth, individuals can lead more balanced and fulfilling lives, while also fostering an environment that encourages growth in those around them.

At the heart of continuous growth is an openness to change and a proactive approach to personal and professional development. This openness involves recognizing that change is a constant and that adaptability is key to navigating life's uncertainties. Embracing change means being willing to step out of comfort zones, take calculated risks, and face challenges head-on. Such a mindset encourages individuals to seek opportunities for learning—whether through formal education, professional experiences, or personal pursuits. By actively engaging in these opportunities, individuals can expand their skill sets, broaden their perspectives, and enhance their overall capabilities.

Resilience is another vital component of continuous growth. The ability to bounce back from setbacks, learn from failures, and maintain a positive outlook in the face of adversity is essential for sustained development. Resilience allows individuals to view challenges not as insurmountable obstacles but as opportunities for growth and learning. When faced with difficulties, resilient individuals can assess the situation, adapt their strategies, and move forward with renewed determination. This capacity to recover and thrive in challenging circumstances not only contributes to personal growth but also sets a powerful example for others, fostering a culture of resilience and growth within communities and workplaces. The commitment to continuous growth encourages lifelong learning. This concept extends beyond formal education and professional development; it encompasses all aspects of life, including emotional, social, and spiritual growth. Lifelong learners are curious individuals who seek to understand themselves and the world around them more deeply. They actively pursue knowledge and experiences that enrich their lives and contribute to their personal evolution. This mindset cultivates a sense of purpose, as individuals align their growth pursuits with their values, passions, and aspirations. As they evolve, they become more equipped to navigate the complexities of life and contribute meaningfully to their communities.

In addition to benefiting individuals, continuous growth also has a ripple effect, influencing those around us. When we actively engage in our own development and embrace a growth-oriented mindset, we create a supportive environment that inspires others to do the same. This collaborative spirit fosters a sense of community, where individuals uplift and motivate one another to pursue their goals. As we share our experiences, lessons learned, and growth journeys, we contribute to a collective consciousness that values learning, resilience, and empowerment. Ultimately, understanding and embracing continuous growth allows us to lead fulfilling lives while positively impacting the world around us.

How Beliefs and Mindsets Influence Continuous Growth

Beliefs and mindsets play a crucial role in shaping our ability to grow continuously. They influence how we perceive challenges, approach obstacles, and engage with the world around us. By understanding the profound impact that beliefs and mindsets have on our behavior, we can begin to harness their power to create lasting change and empowerment in our lives.

Beliefs

Belief is deeply ingrained perceptions that we accept as truth, often without questioning their validity. These beliefs shape our identity, influence our actions, and determine what we think is possible. They can manifest in both empowering and limiting ways. For example, beliefs rooted in self-doubt or fear can hinder growth, while empowering beliefs support self-confidence, motivation, and a desire to take on challenges.

Strengthening empowering beliefs creates a mental framework that supports our goals and promotes personal growth. These beliefs fuel our motivation and determination, enabling us to seize opportunities, pursue success, and approach challenges with resilience and curiosity.

Mindset and Continuous Growth

Mindset is another powerful factor in shaping our behavior. It determines how we perceive opportunities and obstacles, and how we respond to the challenges that arise in our lives. A growth mindset, which emphasizes learning and adaptability, empowers us to view setbacks as opportunities for development rather than failures.

A growth mindset promotes resilience, creativity, and the ability to learn from mistakes. It equips us to approach challenges with determination and curiosity, viewing them as valuable learning experiences that contribute to our personal growth. Cultivating a growth mindset fosters a more adaptable and resilient approach to life's challenges, enabling us to flourish in a rapidly changing world.

The Continuous Growth Journey

The journey of continuous growth requires self-awareness, commitment, and a willingness to challenge deeply rooted perceptions. By recognizing how our beliefs and mindsets influence our behavior, we can harness the brain's potential to create lasting change and empowerment.

Embracing Change and Uncertainty

Change and uncertainty are inevitable parts of life, and embracing them is a key component of the continuous growth journey. By adopting a positive attitude toward change, we empower ourselves to pursue growth and success with confidence.

Consider the following strategies for embracing change and uncertainty:

- **Embrace the Learning Process:** Approach change with curiosity and determination, valuing effort and perseverance over immediate results. View setbacks as opportunities for learning and growth.
- **Foster Curiosity:** Cultivate a sense of curiosity and creativity by exploring new ideas and perspectives. Embrace different experiences and viewpoints to expand your understanding of the world.
- **Embrace Failure:** See failure as a stepping stone to success, using the lessons learned from setbacks to inform future actions. Reflect on these experiences to guide your personal growth.

Pursuing Personal and Collective Growth

Personal and collective growth are intertwined, as individual development contributes to the growth of the community around us. By setting growth-oriented goals and focusing on development rather than mere performance, we can ensure that our journey of continuous growth remains aligned with our values and aspirations.

To pursue personal and collective growth, consider these strategies:

- **Set Growth-Oriented Goals:** Establish goals that reflect your values and aspirations, focusing on development rather than achievement alone. Use these goals as benchmarks for personal progress and collective success.
- **Prioritize Lifelong Learning:** Engage in continuous learning by seeking new knowledge and experiences that challenge and expand your perspectives. Lifelong learning is a cornerstone of both personal fulfillment and collective growth.

The path to continuous growth is an ongoing process of self-discovery, empowerment, and transformation. By embracing this journey, we can unlock our potential, cultivate resilience, and create a life that is truly aligned with our deepest values and aspirations.

Lifelong learning is essential for personal and collective empowerment. It's about constantly seeking new knowledge, skills, and experiences to enrich ourselves and contribute to the growth of those around us. When we embrace learning as a tool for development, we unlock endless possibilities for personal transformation. Engaging in educational opportunities, whether formal or informal, empowers us to evolve and adapt in a rapidly changing world.

In addition to personal growth, contributing to collective growth fosters a sense of community and belonging. When we participate in activities and initiatives that align with our values, we not only nurture our own development but also uplift those around us. This collaborative approach to growth creates an environment where everyone thrives, and our contributions leave a lasting impact.

The Impact of Continuous Growth on Personal Empowerment

Continuous growth profoundly influences personal empowerment, enhancing our ability to pursue goals, overcome challenges, and achieve fulfillment. By committing to lifelong learning and development, we can create lives that resonate with our values and aspirations, promoting resilience and empowerment.

Pursuing Goals and Aspirations

A mindset centered on continuous growth equips us with the confidence and determination to pursue our goals and dreams. By focusing on personal development, we overcome limiting beliefs and self-doubt, allowing us to seize opportunities for success.

To effectively pursue your goals while fostering growth, consider these strategies:

- **Set growth-oriented goals:** Align your goals with your values and focus on development rather than simply performance. Let your objectives serve as a roadmap for personal achievement and transformation.
- **Embrace the learning process:** Value effort and perseverance over immediate results. Approach your journey with curiosity, treating setbacks as opportunities to learn and grow.

- **Celebrate progress:** Acknowledge your successes and the effort you put into achieving them. Use each milestone as motivation to continue moving toward your goals with enthusiasm.

Overcoming Challenges and Setbacks

Continuous growth provides us with the tools to face challenges and setbacks with resilience and adaptability. By adopting a growth oriented mindset, we can view obstacles as opportunities for growth, learning valuable lessons that inspire future actions.

To navigate challenges with a growth mindset, try these approaches:

- **Embrace change and uncertainty:** Recognize that change brings new learning opportunities. Use uncertainty as a catalyst for expanding your understanding and skills.
- **Use adaptive coping strategies:** Manage stress and adversity by focusing on problem-solving and emotion regulation. This helps you respond to challenges in constructive ways.
- **Promote resilience:** Cultivate resilience by fostering a positive mindset and using setbacks as stepping stones for growth. Approach difficulties with confidence, seeing them as opportunities to strengthen your character.

Future Directions

The power of continuous growth is transformative, shaping both our personal lives and the world around us. By recognizing how beliefs and mindsets influence our behavior, we can harness this power to overcome limiting beliefs, build resilience, and achieve our goals. This journey requires dedication, courage, and a willingness to challenge beliefs that no longer serve us.

As you embark on this journey of growth and self-discovery, it's crucial to nurture self-awareness, compassion, and resilience. By embracing your true self and reframing your limiting beliefs, you can build a life aligned with your values and aspirations. The path to empowerment is an ongoing process, offering endless opportunities for personal and collective growth.

In the following chapters, we'll delve deeper into how to realize your infinite potential. You'll explore the influence of beliefs and mindsets on your actions and gain practical tools and techniques to create a life that reflects your values and goals. Through self-awareness, introspection, and a commitment to growth, you'll unlock your potential and begin your journey toward self-determination.

EMBRACING YOUR LIMITLESS POTENTIAL

The journey of personal growth and self-determination is an ongoing, ever-evolving process that extends far beyond achieving any singular goal or milestone. It is about developing a mindset that embraces lifelong learning, self-awareness, and the ability to adapt and evolve. This journey demands more than just ambition—it requires the courage to confront limitations, both real and imagined, and the commitment to consistently pursue personal evolution. Whether we are navigating the complexities of our relationships, careers, or inner emotional landscapes, this path is marked by moments of reflection, trial, and triumph. As we challenge the constraints that we or society have placed upon us, we unlock new levels of potential and open doors to greater fulfillment.

At the core of this journey lies the transformative power of belief—specifically, the belief in one's limitless potential. Beliefs shape how we view the world and ourselves, acting as the foundation for the decisions we make and the actions we take. When we begin to shift away from self-limiting beliefs and instead cultivate empowering beliefs that affirm our capabilities, we transform not only our internal mindset but also our external reality. By embracing the notion that we are capable of achieving far more than we ever imagined, we begin to lead a life of meaning, purpose, and achievement. The act of believing in our potential enables us to live authentically, pursue our passions, and overcome challenges with resilience and determination.

Understanding Infinite Potential

Having limitless potential means recognizing that there are no fixed boundaries to your abilities, growth, or achievements. It embodies the belief that you can continuously evolve, learn, and adapt throughout your life, regardless of the obstacles or setbacks you face. Limitless potential is not about being perfect or achieving everything at once, but about understanding that your capacity for growth is boundless. By embracing a mindset of openness and curiosity, you unlock new possibilities and opportunities, allowing you to reach beyond what you once thought was possible.

Infinite potential is the profound understanding that our abilities, opportunities, and capacity for growth are not static; they are ever-changing and adaptable. This recognition allows us to see life as an open field of possibilities rather than a set of fixed outcomes. The idea of infinite potential is grounded in the belief that each of us has the power to shape our own experiences, transforming our dreams into reality through continuous learning, self-improvement, and intentional effort. Rather than being bound by past limitations or the circumstances we were born into, we are free to evolve and expand in ways that align with our desires and goals.

Embracing the idea that our potential is limitless, we begin to view challenges not as roadblocks but as opportunities for growth. Each experience—whether a success or a failure—adds to our understanding of ourselves and our world, pushing us toward new levels of achievement. Our capabilities grow as we take on new challenges, learn new skills, and expand our horizons. This ongoing process of growth is fueled by self-determination, a belief in our ability to overcome obstacles, and the courage to push past the comfort zones that often limit us. In this way, infinite potential is not just about the outcomes we achieve but about the mindset we cultivate, one that is always open to learning, evolving, and becoming more.

When we embrace our infinite potential, we also commit to a journey of personal transformation. This journey requires us to let go of self-limiting beliefs—those internal narratives that tell us we aren't capable, deserving, or strong enough to achieve the life we want. These beliefs often stem from fear, past failures, or societal conditioning that teaches us to doubt our worth. However, when we choose to replace these limiting beliefs with empowering ones, we create a new internal framework that supports growth, resilience, and empowerment. We begin to understand that we are not defined by the challenges we face but by how we respond to them.

Central to this transformation is the concept of self-determination—the ability to take control of our own destiny and direct our lives in the way we envision. Embracing our infinite potential means recognizing that we are the architects of our future, capable of designing a life that reflects our passions, values, and purpose. It involves setting clear goals, taking actionable steps toward them, and cultivating the perseverance necessary to stay the course, even in the face of obstacles. In doing so, we align ourselves with the infinite possibilities that life offers, opening ourselves up to success, fulfillment, and personal empowerment.

Embracing infinite potential is a powerful act of self-empowerment. It gives us the confidence to pursue our dreams with passion and determination, knowing that we are capable of far more than we initially believed. This belief not only transforms the way we approach our personal and professional lives but also radiates outward, inspiring those around us to recognize and embrace their own infinite potential. By fostering a mindset of continuous growth and self-determination, we unlock doors to new opportunities and create a life filled with purpose, achievement, and boundless possibilities.

How Beliefs and Mindsets Influence Our Infinite Potential

Beliefs and mindsets play a crucial role in shaping our infinite potential. They influence how we perceive challenges, approach obstacles, and interact with the world. When we understand how deeply held beliefs shape our actions, we gain the ability to shift our mindset and create empowering outcomes.

Beliefs and Infinite Possibilities

Beliefs are deeply ingrained perceptions that we often accept as truth without questioning their validity. These beliefs shape our identity, guide our behavior, and dictate what we believe is achievable. Limiting beliefs, such as self-doubt or fear, can restrict our growth and limit our possibilities. Conversely, reinforcing positive beliefs creates a mental framework that supports our goals and fosters self-confidence, motivation, and determination. Empowering beliefs allow us to pursue opportunities for success and approach challenges with curiosity and resilience.

Mindset and Infinite Possibilities

Mindset is a powerful determinant of behavior. It shapes how we perceive challenges, cope with obstacles, and engage with the world. A growth mindset is key to unlocking our infinite potential. It fosters adaptability, resilience, and a willingness to learn from mistakes, enabling us to see challenges as opportunities for growth. Cultivating a growth mindset equips us with an empowered approach to life, helping us break free from limiting beliefs and embrace a future filled with growth, development, and resilience.

Embrace Your Infinite Potential

Embracing your infinite potential requires self-awareness, commitment, and the courage to challenge deeply rooted perceptions. By recognizing how beliefs and mindsets impact behavior, you can harness your brain's power to create lasting change and empowerment.

Nurturing Empowering Beliefs

Nurturing empowering beliefs is vital to embracing your infinite potential. These beliefs enable you to face challenges with determination and view them as opportunities for growth. Consider the following strategies to cultivate empowering beliefs:

- **Challenge Limiting Beliefs:** Identify and question limiting beliefs about your abilities. Explore alternative perspectives that align with empowering and optimistic beliefs.
- **Adopt Positive Self-Talk:** Use positive affirmations and self-talk to focus on your strengths, accomplishments, and potential for growth.
- **Strengthen Beliefs:** Reinforce empowering beliefs through consistent practice. Use visualization, positive self-talk, and gratitude to embed new, empowering beliefs into your mindset.

Build Confidence and Self-Esteem

Building confidence and self-esteem is key to unlocking your infinite potential. It empowers you to seize opportunities for growth with confidence and resilience. Consider the following strategies to build your confidence and self-esteem:

- **Set Achievable Goals:** Break down larger goals into smaller, manageable tasks, and celebrate your progress along the way.
- **Reflect on Achievements:** Regularly acknowledge and reflect on your accomplishments to reinforce a sense of capability and success.
- **Practice Self-Compassion:** Treat yourself with kindness, especially during setbacks. Self-compassion promotes resilience and helps you maintain confidence in challenging situations.

By embracing these practices and cultivating a growth mindset, you open yourself to infinite possibilities. The journey of self-determination and personal growth is an ongoing process, one that empowers you to realize your full potential and create a life of meaning, fulfillment, and success.

It is essential to celebrate your successes and achievements, no matter how big or small. Acknowledge the value of your efforts and perseverance, recognizing that each accomplishment brings you one step closer to your goals. Celebrating these victories not only boosts your motivation but also reinforces the belief that you are capable of achieving greatness. Use each success as a driving force to continue pursuing your aspirations and dreams with renewed determination and confidence.

Show Self-Compassion

In times of stress and adversity, practicing self-compassion becomes a vital tool for maintaining mental and emotional well-being. Self-compassion means treating yourself with the same kindness, care, and understanding that you would offer a loved one. It's about recognizing that you, too, are human and that making mistakes, facing setbacks, and experiencing hardship is a natural part of life's journey. Instead of harshly judging yourself for your perceived shortcomings, self-compassion encourages you to be gentle and patient. This practice helps reduce feelings of guilt or inadequacy and replaces them with a sense of empathy for your own struggles.

Prioritizing your well-being is not a luxury but a necessity for building resilience. When you make time for self-care—whether it's through rest, reflection, or engaging in activities that nurture your spirit—you strengthen your mental and physical health, better equipping yourself to handle life's challenges. Self-compassion also involves embracing vulnerability. It allows you to acknowledge your emotions without feeling overwhelmed by them, fostering emotional balance and providing the strength to persevere. By showing yourself compassion, you create a foundation of inner strength, allowing you to face difficulties with grace, patience, and determination.

Cultivate Gratitude

Gratitude is a transformative practice that shifts your focus from what you lack to the abundance that already exists in your life. It encourages you to pause and reflect on the positive aspects of your journey, from your achievements and strengths to the support and opportunities around you. By cultivating gratitude, you actively nurture a mindset of appreciation, which can enhance your overall well-being. This shift in perspective not only boosts your mood but also fosters optimism, helping you see possibilities where there may have once been doubt or fear. Gratitude allows you to celebrate your progress and stay motivated, even when faced with challenges.

Beyond its immediate emotional benefits, gratitude also plays a key role in personal growth. When you focus on the blessings in your life, you develop a stronger sense of purpose and contentment. Gratitude helps to deepen your connection with others, as you express appreciation for the people who support and inspire you. It also encourages you to view challenges as opportunities for learning and growth, as you recognize the lessons they offer. By embracing a grateful heart, you open yourself to new opportunities, approach life with greater enthusiasm, and cultivate a positive, forward-looking mindset that attracts further success and fulfillment.

How Infinite Potential Impacts Personal Growth

Embracing your infinite potential has a profound impact on your personal growth. It opens the door to greater possibilities, enabling you to pursue your goals with confidence and resilience. By recognizing your limitless potential, you align your life with your core values and aspirations, fostering a sense of fulfillment and purpose.

When you believe in your ability to grow and evolve, you become empowered to face challenges, overcome setbacks, and achieve success.

Pursue Your Goals and Aspirations

When you embrace your infinite potential, you can pursue your goals with a sense of purpose and determination. A growth-minded approach allows you to move beyond self-doubt and limiting beliefs, opening up opportunities for development and success. Set goals that align with your values and focus on personal growth, not just performance.

To pursue your goals with an infinite mindset, consider the following strategies:

- **Set growth-minded goals:** Focus on setting goals that reflect your values and aspirations, emphasizing growth and development rather than solely on outcomes. Use your goals as a guide for personal achievement and fulfillment.

- **Embrace the learning process:** Value effort and perseverance over immediate success. Approach your goals with curiosity and a willingness to learn from setbacks, viewing challenges as opportunities for growth.

- **Celebrate progress:** Take time to celebrate your progress along the way. Acknowledge the effort and dedication it takes to keep moving forward, using your successes as motivation to continue striving toward your dreams.

Overcome Challenges and Setbacks

Embracing your infinite potential also means developing the resilience to overcome challenges and setbacks. A growth-oriented approach allows you to see difficulties as opportunities for learning and growth. With this mindset, every obstacle becomes a stepping stone toward a deeper understanding of yourself and the world.

To overcome challenges with resilience, consider these strategies:

- **Embrace change and uncertainty:** Welcome change and uncertainty as part of the growth process. These moments offer opportunities for self-discovery and personal evolution.

- **Use adaptive coping strategies:** Focus on problem-solving and emotional regulation to manage stress. Developing adaptive coping mechanisms equips you to navigate adversity with grace.

- **Promote resilience:** Cultivate a positive mindset that supports your ability to recover from setbacks. Approach challenges with confidence and use each experience as a lesson to fuel future growth.

Future Directions

Harnessing your infinite potential is a transformative force that can shape both your life and the world around you. By understanding how your beliefs and mindset influence your actions, you gain the power to overcome limiting beliefs, build resilience, and achieve your goals. This journey requires courage, commitment, and a willingness to confront beliefs that no longer serve you.

As you embark on this journey, it is important to cultivate self-awareness, compassion, and resilience. By embracing your true self and reframing limiting beliefs, you align your life with your values and aspirations. The path to self-determination is a continuous process of learning, growth, and transformation that offers endless opportunities for personal and collective evolution.

Embrace the Power of Faith

The journey of personal growth and self-determination is a lifelong endeavor, marked by continuous learning, self-discovery, and transformation. It requires courage, commitment, and a willingness to challenge and change limiting beliefs. At the heart of this journey lies the power of faith—faith in yourself, in your potential, and in your ability to create a meaningful and fulfilling life.

As you reach the end of this journey, remember that the power of belief resides within you. It is a force that can be harnessed to create the life you envision and deserve. Embrace the journey, trust the process, and unleash the infinite potential that lies within you.

Thank you for embarking on this journey of personal growth and empowerment. May your path be filled with joy, fulfillment, and endless possibilities.